A GUIDE TO
GOOD WINE

Le dégorgeur
An intricate operation in the making of Champagne

A GUIDE TO
GOOD WINE

Contributions by
ALLAN SICHEL, LESLIE SEYD, H. B. LANSON,
LANCE K. COCK, IAN MACKENZIE,
ALFRED LANGENBACH.

With an Introduction by
J. W. MAHONEY, LL.B.,
The Wine & Spirit Association of Great Britain

REVISED EDITION
EDITOR: BRIAN DOUGHTY

ABBEY LIBRARY
LONDON

© MURRAYS BOOK SALES (KING'S CROSS) LTD
FIRST PUBLISHED 1952
SECOND EDITION 1959
THIRD EDITION 1970
THIS EDITION 1971

Contents

List of Illustrations

PHOTOGRAPHS

WOODCUTS

MAPS

LINE DRAWINGS

Note

GOOD wine needs no bush. But unless one can tell a good wine on seeing, smelling or tasting it, it may hide its light under a bushel.

This book tries to explain what good wine is, where and how it is made, and how to buy, keep, serve and enjoy it. Wiser books about wine have been written, but none, perhaps, as expert as this for the purpose. The authors have been renowned members of the wine-trade, whose opinions merit the same respect as the famous wines with which their names are associated. Any errors, indeed, are the fault of the editor, and have arisen in the task of co-ordinating so many diverse and sometimes surprising opinions into a harmonious whole.

The editor wishes to thank his contributors for their generosity; the many wine syndicates, here and abroad, for advice and illustrations; the Keeper of Printed Books, The British Museum, for permission to reproduce the woodcuts; the Curators of the National Gallery and the Victoria and Albert Museum; Mr. William MacQuitty; and Mr. Sydney Barnson, who really conceived the work and provided constant inspiration.

A. R. T.

This book is not intended as an Encyclopeadia and, for example does not set out to list every Chateau or commune although all the main ones are indicated together with some lesser known establishments. Rather does it seek to provide a general grounding in the basic knowledge necessary to develop and enhance an interest in one of the noblest pleasures open to man.

B.D.

Introduction

WHY drink wine? In this book the reader, whatever the present extent of his knowledge of one of the most interesting and varied subjects of civilised culture, will find a great deal to instruct and to elevate him. Articles on different wines written by some of the foremost British experts on each wine, men who spend their working lives and gain their livelihood by their knowledge of the produce of the vine, men whose forebears have been in the wine trade for generations, cannot fail to convey something which is lacking from the works of gifted amateurs. No man in the wine trade, whether here or abroad, pretends to be an expert on all wines, and none would write about all; so that the system of arrangement of this book by which one man deals with one class of wine does give the reader the advantage of expert knowledge to the highest degree.

The introductory chapters deal briefly with the history of the vine and the general theory and practice of the production of wine, including a simple chemical analysis of the constituents of wine and an account of the process of fermentation. Inevitably, the following chapters, dealing with individual types of wines, must be confined mainly to the European vineyards; for, although wine did not originate in Europe and can be made in any part of the world where the climate allows for the commercial cultivation of the vine, it is in Europe that the art and process of wine production has reached its highest pitch. In the older wine-producing countries outside Europe, production has been mainly for local consumption, in large quantities, of a standard article, and little effort has been made to produce small quantities of excellent quality wines on a par with those which we associate with such countries as France and Germany. In the New World, where, also, the vine is grown commercially, the knowledge and appreciation of wine is steadily and rapidly increasing, but in general the wines are mainly copies of the better-known European wines, and, so far as the writer knows, none of the new countries has yet produced a native wine with its own special characteristics and qualities which will bear comparison with the choicest growths of the Old World. An Australian burgundy, a South African hock, a Chilean *riesling* may all be wines of excellent quality and flavour, but they cannot be an exact copy of their European counterparts, for the conditions of growth in Europe cannot be duplicated. The same grape, the same method of cultivation, the same method of production may be used, but the grower cannot duplicate the exact soil conditions or the distribution and amount of sun, rain and wind, and these will always cause differences which will be reflected in the final product.

It is argued, and perhaps with some justice, that we unconsciously set up European wines as a standard against which all others are measured, and that we class the latter as good or bad in direct proportion to the degree to which they imitate European wines. I do not, however, think this criticism is completely justified, and I am sure that, if the newer—or even some of the lesser-known older—countries should produce an independent type of wine, it would be judged on its merits by the trade and by the consumer. In fact, I have quite frequently come across wines which are unusual but attractive, and would be acceptable to the consumer if he could be induced to try them. The last phrase is the governing factor. The wine lover is ultra-conservative, and it takes a lot to induce him to change from his old favourites to something new, however good it may be. It follows, therefore, that the newer countries have felt bound to offer the consumer something resembling the product of the older countries. They are quite alive to the difficulties and disadvantages of this procedure, and are undoubtedly trying to strike out on a new line with quite different national wines—but, unfortunately, it must be a slow business. Until they have succeeded, however, it is inevitable that any book on wine must deal mainly with the European vineyards, and that the remarks made therein apply, *mutatis mutandis*, to the vineyards of the New World.

In Great Britain, wine was a luxury, to be taken, except by the fortunate few, only on occasions of celebration or rejoicing. In wine-producing countries, it is the usual daily drink of the man in the street, and by far the greater part of all the wine made is consumed locally. There is no accident about this. We were formerly amongst the world's largest consumers of claret, and we consumed correspondingly large quantities of other wines; but the vicious taxation to which all distilled and fermented beverages are now subject had quite killed the daily wine-drinking habit, and had put wine out of the reach of most people, except for rare occasions. If it were not for this taxation, there is no reason why wine should have lost its old popularity with us, for it has everything in its favour and little against. Its alcohol content is generally so small that it does not affect the ordinary drinker; it is chemically pure and antiseptic and free from germs as a result of its alcohol content; and it is the drink which, of all beverages, is perhaps nearest to nature. In the production of wine, man does little except crush the grapes so that fermentation may take its natural course, and then care for and purify the wine until it is ready for consumption. It cannot be emphasised too strongly that wine is a completely natural drink provided by Mother Nature herself freely and abundantly, and it is accepted as such in all wine-producing countries. Why it should be singled out for penal taxation in other countries is a mystery which nobody has yet solved. Why we should import grapes at high prices plus import taxes, and not grape-juice at low prices without taxes, is something the wine-lover cannot understand!

Literally thousands of millions of gallons of wine are consumed annually, of which we in Great Britain account for only a very small portion! The greater part of it is drunk for the primary purpose of quenching thirst. It is drunk in preference to water because the whole history of mankind proves that man is not satisfied with water and always asks for something more—and that something more is generally a distilled or fermented liquor. Originally, perhaps, there was sound reasoning behind this, for the purity of water was suspect and a germ-free drink, such as wine, was essential. To-day science has made our water safe, and there has been a considerable growth—even in wine-producing countries—of germ-proof non-alcoholic liquors competing for the patronage of the consumer. It will be interesting to see, as the years go on, whether the distilled or fermented alcoholic liquor will yield place to the non-alcoholic, chemical, man-made soft drink, and, if it does, there is little doubt that the blame will be on the shoulders of the tax collector. But it is difficult to believe that beverages with thousands of years of use and enjoyment behind them, beverages traditionally associated with the art of living, the inspiration of the poet and the warrior, the solace of the sick, the ill and the weary, the source of wit and laughter and love, will really be defeated by the onslaught of the chemist with his essences and acids.

Whether wine is really beneficial to the human organism is a question which may never be decided. The analyst will tell us that it is a drink which is chemically pure, and that it contains certain proportions of acids, sugars, minerals, etc., which are present in too small a concentration to be of any use in feeding the body. But the wine-lover would never yield the last word on this subject to the scientist or the analyst. He will claim that the natural produce of the sunny southern vineyards, the produce of the sun and the rain and the soil, contains the virtues of the natural elements which gave it life, and the concentrated warmth and fire of the sun, which are incapable of analysis in the present state of our knowledge. He will tell you that the regular wine-drinker lives longer and suffers from fewer ailments than his teetotal brother, that wine builds him up after an illness, that it kills germs in the blood, that it acts as a mild antiseptic. The number of medicinal properties attributed to wine are legion, and perhaps we might say that it is a wise man who pays heed to tradition and long-held beliefs, to the accumulated experience of bygone centuries, and does not dismiss it as false because it is incapable of scientific explanation. The production of wine is an art, not a science, and we cannot necessarily explain its results. But this is, of course, a purely incidental exploration of the qualities of wine. We do not drink wine in the ordinary way because we think it will be good for us—we drink it because we like it, and because we are always finding some new enjoyment in it.

Wine is the beverage which is the natural complement of the foods we most enjoy and appreciate. Experience has shown that wines and foods have certain natural affinities for each other, and are found at their best in combination. The wine stimulates the gastric juices, brings out the flavour and savour of the food, and aids digestion, whilst the food brings out the finest qualities of the wine by contrast and comparison. Together they are the perfect combination, exceeding in gustatory value the sum of the separate constituents, and together they give the reason and the excuse for the large or small banquets which form one of the highest expressions of our culture and our civilisation. But in spite of its pre-eminent place in the art of living, wine is, in itself, essentially simple. It may have been—perhaps still is— associated with ritual and tradition and ceremonial, and the advanced wine lover dearly appreciates those little refinements in service and consumption which give wine a halo of mystery; but they are not essential. There are certain conventions, culled from the preferences of centuries of wine-lovers, that certain wines shall be served with certain dishes, in a certain way or at a certain temperature, and it is indisputable that the wines are then served at their best. But the conventions are not immutable, and if they do not suit you, the best thing is to ignore them. If you prefer port with your oysters, served in a tumbler, or a china mug of well-warmed moselle with your sweet, that is your choice, and no true wine-lover would attempt to influence you to his choice instead of your own. Naturally, however, you cannot assume that your guests will share your rather unusual tastes, and, in entertaining, it is thus a social necessity to follow the generally accepted order and method of service of wines. Nowadays, when meals are less elaborate, the problem is easy to solve, white wine with fish and white meats, red wine with butcher's meat and game, port with the cheese or dessert, sherry as an apéritif—a more detailed list is printed further on in this book. But do remember that the former rigid barriers have largely fallen, and you will find many people—even in the wine trade itself—who will not observe them. If you are doubtful, select a white wine rather than red, or use either champagne or sherry as a beverage wine which may be drunk throughout all courses. Give the wine a chance—have it served properly, decanted if necessary, given the opportunity of stretching itself in the air after its long imprisonment in the bottle, and it will well repay you. Don't serve a delicate wine with any highly flavoured or vinegary dish, for the food will inevitably kill it.

Perhaps I can, in this foreword, give you a few hints of a general nature in the care, service and appreciation of wines. In the following chapters, you will read all about wine in its country of origin, and you will learn as much therefrom as you can ever learn from a written description of something which is essentially a matter of taste and experience. A deep and practical knowledge of wine comes from study and tasting over a period of years, during which the palate and the memory become educated to such an extent that they can place a wine immediately. Such a detailed knowledge is essential for the man who makes his living by wine, but it is not essential for the ordinary consumer, and is rarely, if ever, achieved by him, for he has not the same opportunities as the merchant for study. But although you may not be able to taste a wine and say unhesitatingly "Château Margaux, 1929" or something similar, you can say from your first sip whether you like the wine or not, and for you that is the main criterion. Knowledge and comparison of wine develop over many years, during which you unconsciously absorb knowledge, and, perhaps, raise your standard of taste and appreciation; but a liking for wine can come with the first glass. You may not be able to express your liking in the technical jargon—you may not know the exact shade of meaning intended to be conveyed by the expert when he says that a wine has finesse, or bouquet, or delicacy, or roundness, but you can say what you find in the wine by the use of good, solid Anglo-Saxon expressions of appreciation. If a wine has cleanness and flavour, you will like it, and it is immaterial that somebody else uses some rather roundabout and obscure terms to say the same thing. Of course, I do not mean to say that the technical expressions are mere tricks of the trade or attempts to show superiority by the so-called expert. They do convey fine shades of meaning to the initiate, and the more your palate develops naturally by the consumption of wine, the more grateful you will be for these additional words to mark off the little differences which you will always find even between two wines of the same year and from the same vineyard.

Until you can exercise your own judgment adequately, you should place complete trust in your wine merchant. It is his job to provide you with selected wines of good quality to suit your palate and your pocket, and the great majority of wine merchants discharge this duty well and faithfully, and take a pride in their profession. If you are not satisfied with what he supplies, he will take it back and provide something else. He will always be glad to taste a wine with you, and to discuss its particular character-istics and its virtues or defects before you buy it. He is always anxious to pass on to you the love of wine which he has acquired, and to share with you his many experiences, discoveries and surprises in its study. If he is not this type of wine merchant, you should change him; for half the joy of wine comes from sharing your discoveries with an understanding and sympathetic friend, and gradually finding that you can hold your own in the many arguments which arise between wine-lovers. Such a wine merchant will provide you with a carefully selected, yet moderate and inexpensive, cellar on which you can depend with confidence for all occasions, and will keep it replenished for you at, it is safe to say, increasingly short intervals.

But, you will say, I have no cellar. Few of us have a cellar to-day in the ordinary sense of the word, and no longer can we lay down a pipe of port for our newly-born son's coming-of-age, or make an advantageous purchase of vintage clarets for maturing. To-day, your wine merchant must be your cellarer also, and it is his cellar on which you will draw for all your requirements. A small stock at home you must keep, but you can buy ready-made binning racks which will fit into any empty space in a cupboard or corner, or even into an empty chest of drawers, and thus give you a small cellar of your own. All you have to do is to ensure that your wines are binned horizontally so that the wine is in contact with the cork and air is excluded, and take as much care as possible to see that the temperature is kept even—between 50° and 60° Fahrenheit—and that all draughts, smells, fumes, dampness or any other violent diversion from the normal are avoided. Wines mature slowly, and to reach their best and to stay there, they require everything around them to be slow and gradual and careful. They dislike an excess of heat or cold, of light or draught, any unsavoury smells or violent movement. Do everything slowly and carefully and gently, and you will find that the wine well repays your devotion when the time for consumption arrives. Always remember that wine is a living thing whose development cannot be hurried.

Let us assume that the time has arrived, and that, for an important dinner party, you wish to serve your guests of your best at its best. The wines you drink from day to day are not good enough, and you desire to place the choicest growths and vintages before your guests. First, then, select your food and build up your wine list around the menu, having, for preference, a separate wine specially chosen to accompany each dish. Your own cellar will probably not be large enough for the variety and quantity you require, so the next step is to call on your wine merchant and take him into your confidence. He will pick for you wines, both red and white, which have matured until they have reached their best—ports, vintage or otherwise, sherry, if you desire it for an apéritif, a champagne and the brandy or liqueurs you choose to finish the meal, or, if this is too ambitious, whatever you agree with him is necessary.

A white wine will require little to be done to it before it reaches the table. It should be served chilled to slightly below the room temperature, but be careful not to chill it too much or too rapidly. Then it can be poured straight from the bottle into the glasses. A red wine, however (and even some of the older white wines), may require to be decanted because a sediment has formed in it during its long period of maturation. This must not be allowed to enter the glass and cloud the wine. Therefore, stand the wine up in the room where it is to be consumed, say, twenty-four hours ahead, and let the sediment fall naturally to the bottom. Then draw the cork carefully so that the sediment is not disturbed, wipe the neck, and pour the clear wine slowly from the bottle into the decanter. It is best to have a light behind the bottle as you pour, so that you can see immediately when any of the sediment begins to move to the neck; then stop your decanting, and, if you like, use the remnants for cooking purposes.

Decanting is desirable for any wines which throw a sediment, and is essential for some, including vintage port. It is preferable to the use of a wicker basket or cradle, for, however careful one may be not to shake the bottle unnecessarily, it is inevitable that the sediment is disturbed, and the later glasses poured from the bottle would be contaminated with it.

Your red wines should be served at the room temperature, and left in the dining-room for twenty-four hours beforehand, so as to acquire the temperature naturally. Whether decanted or not, the bottle should be opened some two or three hours before the meal, so as to allow the wine to breathe and develop in the air rapidly, and so as to allow any bottle "stink" to be dissipated. It is quite harmless. Your white wines, including champagnes, and your spirits or liqueurs, do not require this preliminary treatment, but your white wines and champagnes must be chilled before service so that they cause just a little mist to form on the outside of the glass.

A little advice about glasses is also desirable at this stage. First, all your glassware must be perfectly clean and well polished, particularly if it has been washed with any soap powder or detergent, and even more so if, like a decanter, it is difficult to get inside. Ideally, you should have a separate type of glass for practically each wine or spirit, all of good quality and all thin, but nowadays we cannot manage that, and it is quite common to procure a sort of standard glass which can be used for more than one purpose. The ordinary claret-type glass can be used for any type of red wine and most white wines, or even for port and sherry, but you do require the separate type of long-stemmed glass for Alsatians, hocks, etc., and the bowl-type glass for champagne. A small-size liqueur glass is also useful. In practice, you need not pay too much attention to the fetish of special glasses. Glasses do improve the wine and allow it to be shown and served at its best; but wine is your servant, not your master, and it must submit to any type of glassware you find it convenient to use. Do, however, avoid the tumbler type of glass if you possibly can; the stemmed glass does fulfil certain special functions.

When wine is served, it is customary for the host to be helped first with just a little. This he "noses" and tastes, and, if it is satisfactory, the remainder of the guests are then served, ladies first and gentlemen afterwards in a clockwise direction. The host is served last. Follow out this procedure with the second and later bottles, so that the host can pass the wine as satisfactory, and never pour wine from a new bottle into a glass still containing wine from an earlier bottle if it can possibly be avoided—in case the second bottle differs from the first. Do not fill any glass more than two-thirds full, so that the aroma and bouquet may be concentrated in the empty space at the top. If, as the host, you wish to test the wine properly before serving it to your guests, you take the small portion which has been poured into your glass and swirl it round the sides by a wrist motion. Then hold it up to the light and look at its colour, which should, of course, be perfectly clear and brilliant. Then "nose" it, by inhaling deeply its bouquet so as to detect any corky, woody or other smell, and, lastly, take a sip and roll it round your tongue so as to savour it to the full. Only when it has passed all these tests do you give the signal for it to be served to the guests.

Smoking is always a controversial subject with wine drinkers. Smoking to excess, which furs the tongue, obviously destroys temporarily the palate, and you will not then enjoy even the finest wines, but smoking in moderation is not necessarily harmfull. If you are drinking wines of the finest quality, you owe it to them and yourself to have a perfectly clean palate, and therefore should not smoke; but otherwise, you can please yourself. At formal banquets, there will, of course, be no smoking until the chairman has given permission after the Royal Toast, and even then many of the diners will probably prefer to drink their port before lighting up.

Happily, perhaps, you will not drink wines only at public banquets or on special occasions. If you are a true wine-lover, you will drink them with your meals as often as your pocket allows—and you will enjoy your meals all the more. At home, you will probably not serve the oldest and choicest vintages, the château-bottled clarets, the vintage ports, the liqueur brandies and other superlative examples of the art of the viticulturist, but you can still have an excellent bottle of wine at a reasonable price. We do not always travel in a Rolls-Royce; sometimes we go by 'bus or train, but we get there just the same, and we enjoy the Rolls-Royce travel all the more because of the contrast. Not that you decry the ordinary day-to-day wines. Only those which are of good quality and are good value for money are shipped here, but, as in everything else, there are some of superlative quality which you can only taste occasionally because there are not enough of them to go round and because they are necessarily too expensive for daily consumption. In passing, I might add that the quality of a bottle of wine increases far more than in proportion to its price. You have to pay the same for the duty, freight, bottling charges, etc., included in the price, so that any extra shillings you pay go entirely on the wine; one at 12s. may easily be twice as good as one at 10s.—that is, if you can evaluate quality in wines in that way—so that it is always more economical to buy the more expensive wine.

For your ordinary home consumption, ask your wine merchant to recommend some reasonably cheap, home-bottled wines of good quality. He can range the vineyards of the world for you, and it will be surprising if he cannot find something you will like. If price is a major consideration, some of the Empire wines are very attractive and usually cheaper than their Continental counterparts, so that you will not go far wrong. Although the Empire cannot yet pretend to match the finest vintage wines of Europe, the Empire growers can and do produce sound and workmanlike wines which will not disgrace any table, and the saving in cost may allow you to serve them more frequently than you would otherwise do. Do serve wine at your table as often as you can. Wine adds something to a meal—it makes it an occasion. In the words of the French: "A meal without wine is like a day without sunshine." And don't be afraid that a partially used bottle will be wasted. It can always be used in cooking—but I am not going into the question of wine in cooking. If you think it is too precious for that, even low-strength table wines will last for some time, up to say a fortnight, or more if they are transferred to a smaller bottle so that the air cannot get to them. Generally speaking, the older a wine the shorter the time it will remain at its best after it has been opened, but you can easily keep your table wines for a fortnight and your ports and sherries longer. Champagne unfortunately not, for obvious reasons.

It is time I stopped rambling on and on about Wine, but I excuse myself by saying that every wine lover is the same, and never tires of talking and comparing notes on wine. May I finish by reiterating that the study of wine is a subject which is never completely mastered by anyone, that it cannot be reduced to rule or form, and that personal opinions and tastes are a matter of major importance. Only the French have attempted to classify wines in order of quality—in their famous classification of 1855; but they have classified only a few of the best out of the scores of thousands which are found in France, and leave the rest to the judgment of the consumer. After all, how can you classify a wine as being always of a certain quality if you cannot, at the same time, classify the rain and sunshine and climate and soil conditions generally which make the wine good or bad? You must learn to depend on your own palate, and accept a vintage chart or classification as a helpful reminder and not as an infallible guide.

Now read what the experts have to say about the wines they have known and loved almost since infancy.

J. W. MAHONEY

Menu

SUGGESTIONS

(To be discarded or disbelieved at will)

Serve poorer wines before greater, lighter before heavier, younger before older.

Sherry, champagne, hock, mosel or port can accompany an entire meal. Claret and burgundy go with anything except strong fish or egg dishes; luscious white wines go with sweet or fruit.

APERITIF A Fino sherry; champagne; if you must have a cocktail, stick to a Martini.

HORS D'OEUVRES Don't serve a great wine with hors d'oeuvres. The exception is Chablis and oysters—or Sauternes with melon. Suggestions:— dry champagne; light dry mosel; Pouilly-Fuissé; white Graves; Vouvray.

SOUP Light Bordeaux; white Beaujolais; a vin rosé.

FISH Champagne; Meursault; Chablis; Alsace; white Graves; Anjou; Chateauneuf du Pape.

MEAT Light Bordeaux; Beaujolais, Anjou; Alsace; light mosel or Rheingau. Any good red wine with mutton; champagne or burgundy with pork.

POULTRY A good médoc; St. Emilion; burgundy; Chateauneuf; hock or mosel.

GAME Your best red wine—médoc, St. Emilion, Pomerol, Côte des Nuits, a luscious Rhinegau or mosel; try Ch. Cheval Blanc (or Hermitage) with partridge; Romanee-Conti with Pheasant.

DESSERT (and FRUIT) Sauternes; Montrachet; a luscious Rhinegau or mosel.

CHEESE Any wine goes excellently with cheese.

COFFEE Cognac.

Chapter One

The Vine

I

THE vine is a primeval plant, millions of years older than man; but wine is a human creation, and its history is part of the story of civilisation. It is, above all, an embodiment of the European tradition. The roots of the vine are entwined in the roots of society.

In its variety wine, made for the special pleasures of friendship and good company, can suit all tastes and occasions:

> "*Name, Sirs, the wine that most invites your taste;*
> *Champaigne, or Burgundy, or Florence pure,*
> *Or Hock antique, or Lisbon new or old,*
> *Bordeaux, or neat French wine, or Alicant . . .*"

Whatever wine it may be, it is good; for, as the proverb says, "In water you see your own face; in wine the heart of another."

The primitive vine, which flourished in all temperate lands millions of years ago, and of which fossil leaves have been found in Tertiary strata, was not the plant, rich in grape clusters, we know to-day. Its berries were dry and meagre, like peas. It had to wait for man, with his acquired skill in husbandry, to make it bear and flourish. It was developed at a very early date, however, just as our apples, plums, pears and other fruits were, and if care were withdrawn from the cultivation of these, they would soon degenerate into their wild, unfruitful state. "[The] vine," says the Duke of Burgundy in *Henry V*, lamenting the neglect of war, "the merry cheerer of the heart, Unprunèd, dies."

Archæology has revealed the antiquity of the cultivated vine. Grape-stones have been found in Bronze Age tombs. The frescoes in the cave of Tutankhamen show the processes of viticulture, fermentation and cellarage. Earlier still, it seems, the Persian grew grapes for wine, and Persia lays claim to being its first home. Good wine, according to the late Robert Byron in his fine book *The Road to Oxiana*, is still made in Shiraz, and, he adds, some etymologists argue that the name "sherry" comes, not from Jerez de la Frontera, but from the older city. The entire early Mediterranean world ranked the vine high among blessings. The Old Testament distinguishes at least nine different wines—from dry to *liquorous*; their drinking coloured much of the life and literature of the world's youth.

There are several species of vine and many varieties developed from them, but the only indigenous European species is the *Vitis vinifera*, which still grows wild throughout the lower Caucasus. It remains the basic European grape-vine. In the last century, however, the European vineyards were devastated by an American vine-louse, the *Phylloxera*, and it was found necessary, over large areas, to replant with American *Phylloxera*-proof stocks and graft the European varieties on to them.

The vines of Europe are kept small, some three to four feet in height, and are generally trained along poles and wires, so that a vineyard has the appearance of a raspberry garden. In Italy, and in a few other places, they are allowed more liberty, and are strung on wires between trees. To give them plenty of air, they are planted four feet apart, with about five feet between rows to admit of easy ploughing. They are kept periodically pruned, to secure greater vigour in the plants and to maintain the fruit-bearing portion, not in the extreme branches only, but also near the ground. The best grapes, some say, are those nearest to the soil. The berries of wine grapes are much smaller and fleshier than table varieties. They are both black and white. White wine is made from both, but red wine from black grapes only.

The best wine grapes often grow close to the ground

DOMAINE DE MONT-REDON
Châteauneuf-du-Pape

The vine thrives in poor soil. The big flints in this Rhône vineyard add a unique
quality to the wine

A fine old vine of the Douro

A neat and well-kept Bordeaux vineyard

harvest

A bucket of newly-gathered grapes

Gathering grapes

II

There are three general conditions essential to the production of high-quality wine grapes: the right soil, the right amount of sun and the right amount of air.

Vines require a special soil for their best growth. In it most cultivated crops would wither and die. It must be light, sandy, gravelly, stony or chalky—in short, a poor soil. A rich or heavy medium will never produce great wines. No wonder the vine was cherished by our primitive ancestors, when it grew best on desert land! This soil factor, however, now limits the production of really great wines to a few happy corners of Europe: the Bordelais, Côte d'Or and Champagne districts in France; the Rheingau and Mosel in Germany; the Douro in Portugal; the Jerez district in Spain. Good wine is made in great quantity elsewhere, but it can never rank with claret, burgundy, hock, port or sherry.

The soil of the Médoc, home of claret, for instance, is sandy; that of Graves is a mixture of sand and gravel; Champagne is chalky; the Douro slopes can hardly be said to have a soil at all, rather a flaky, broken schist; while Jerez has a burnt calcareous earth called "albariza."

If soil is important, so is sun, and its negative counterparts, rain and frost. But even given a suitable climate, much depends on the actual siting of the vineyard. Vines grown on a south-facing slope may produce quite a different wine from similar vines on a north-facing one. The farther north in Europe vines are grown, the more important the choice of position becomes, since the sun's strength lessens. Position determines, for example, the superiority of the Rheingau district in Germany, where the stony vine-slopes on the north bank of the Rhine face and catch all the summer sunshine, and are happily prevented by a nearby range from enduring the northern winds.

Vines require a lot of air for ventilation. For this reason, many vineyards are situated on hill-slopes, on terraces open to the winds. The best wines of the Douro, for instance, are not grown in the fertile valley, but high on the steep, airy hill-sides. The same feature can be found in the Jerez district, or on the Côte d'Or. The low-lying Médoc is an exception, but there the nearness of the Atlantic gives the necessary ventilation.

Many varieties of vine have been developed from the *Vitis vinifera*, each in special relation to the individual soil and climatic conditions of its region. Of these, a few have attained perfection. They are perfect, however, for their own area only. Transplanted to a different soil, a different climate, they might produce only a mediocre imitation of the wine of their original region. That is why it is inaccurate to talk of Australian burgundy or South African sherry. These countries can produce good, even excellent, wines, but they should be given their own names and not be compared with the great European prototypes.

Among the most famous vines, the Cabernet-Sauvignon, the Pinot, the Riesling and the Palomino stand supreme. These are the vines of the finest claret, burgundy, hock and sherry. Where they are grown, quality is obtained at the expense of quantity, for they give a much lighter harvest than their bourgeois rivals. But they are supreme only in their own regions.

These are the chief factors in the art of viticulture. In addition, there must be constant care and the intelligent continuation of a tradition. Wine makers are rightly conservative, though far from reactionary. There is the story of the Scottish distiller who refused to install a new still lest he spoil his whisky; when he was finally forced to build one, he called in expert coppersmiths to copy exactly the old still, in every bolt, in every joint, and, what is more, in every patch. The whisky retained its quality! Something of that spirit serves a vineyard proprietor well, and the result is the maintenance of a very high standard of wine.

Wine is a living thing. It is made, not only of grapes and yeasts, but of skill and patience. When drinking it, remember that to the making of that wine has gone, not only the labour and care of years, but the experience of centuries. Each glass of wine is a reaffirmation of the real culture of Europe.

A NUREMBERG GLASS OF 1594

Chapter Two

How Wine is Made

THERE are three main phases in the production of wine: the cultivation of the vines, the gathering and fermenting of the grapes and the care of wine after fermentation.

As soon as one year's vintage is over, next year's cultivation begins. If *Phylloxera*-free, grafted vines are being used, any tendrils from the stock must be cut off. Then follow the pruning and restaking of the vines, and sometimes the manuring of them. Phosphate manures are little used. In the Côte d'Or, in older days, fresh earth from the hill-tops was used to restore the vineyard soil, and the pits where it was dug can still be seen. Then, throughout the spring and early summer, the earth is repeatedly hoed, to keep it free from weeds, and to keep the topsoil light and absorbent against later drought. The vines, at intervals, are sulphured and sprayed with chemicals to ward off blight.

A fine harvest is a chancy thing. So much can happen to spoil the perfect ripening of the grapes that a vineyard owner's life makes that of an ordinary farmer seem like a sinecure. There is no room here to number the many vagaries of weather that can ruin the year's work. In order to describe the wine-making processes, we must assume that the grapes ripen well and are heavy in grape-sugar.

The Harvest

The grape harvest takes place in September or October; the farther north the later the harvest. The exact date of beginning is of great importance, and in most cases its choice is left to the experience of the proprietor. Every day waited means a riper grape but involves a greater danger of rain. Most grapes are picked the instant they are ripe; in some cases, however, where a sweet wine is to be made, the harvest is delayed until the grapes are beginning to rot. The outstanding example is that of Sauternes, where the grapes are picked in a state of rottenness.

As the grapes ripen in the sun, an important thing happens. Microscopic spores, or fungi, called *Saccharomycetes*, settle on the skins from the air. These spores have a vital part to play in the making of wine. They settle in millions on the skins, in an attempt to get at the grape-sugar in the juice, on which they would feed. The grapes must not be gathered until it is judged that the saccharomycetes have settled in sufficient quantity. The harvest then takes place with all speed, because rain would, to a large extent, wash off these tiny spores. If there is rain during the harvest, gathering is held up till the vines have had a chance to dry.

Harvesting is done by peasants from the district and from farther afield. The work is very hard, and, in the Douro area, for example, only the local peasants can stand the strain of the three weeks' work of gathering and pressing. The pickers live on the estates, get a little money, food, wine and all the grapes they want, and, in spite of the work, treat the harvest as a holiday.

In most areas the berries are clipped off the vines and loaded directly on to carts to be taken to the châteaux. In some areas, however, a selection is made on the spot. In this way the best and the poorer berries are gathered separately, and wines of corresponding quality produced from each. Bad berries would, if mixed with good, lower the quality of the finest wine. Such selection is very strictly carried out in Germany, where the wines are classed by the quality of the grapes from which they are made. There only the good, ripe berries are picked, and all others left till they in turn become ripe. The vintagers, therefore, work over the same vines day after day, till all the grapes have been picked. A selection on the spot takes place also in Champagne. Sherry grapes, too, must be heavy in grape-sugar. They are, however, picked when ripe, and then left on straw mats to ripen still further in the sun.

Pressing

When the grapes have been taken to the château, or the place where the wine is to be made, they are sometimes separated from the stalks before pressing. This operation is called, in France, *égrappage*, and is usually done by a mechanical sieve. Sometimes, however, the stalks are retained, to give more body to the wine.

The methods of pressing are varied in the different regions; only the principles can be given here.

Pressing is carried out for two main reasons: to free the grape-juice from the skins, pips and flesh, and to enable the saccharomycetes to get at the grape-sugar in the juice and ferment it. The saccharomycetes, which are the yeasts that cause fermentation, turn the grape-juice—the must, as it is called—into wine by converting its grape-sugar into ethyl alcohol and carbon dioxide.

In Bordeaux, the presses are in many cases placed on a level above the vats, or *cuves*. Under pressure the grapes burst their skins and the juice runs out into the *cuves*. This grape-juice makes the *premier vin*. The grapes are then further pressed, and the juice or must extracted goes to make the *vins de presse*—wines of rather poorer quality. A similar system is employed in the other wine districts. Each pressing produces a wine of poorer quality than the previous one.

In Champagne, the law forbids proprietors to extract more than a fixed amount of must from given quantities of grapes. This ensures the high quality of the resultant wine. Furthermore, the poorer wine obtained from the later pressings is not allowed to be called "champagne."

In the Douro, pressing is carried out by the vintagers dancing on the grapes bare-footed. The gentle pressure of the feet bursts the grape-skins and allows the juice to run out, but does not crush the pips of the berries. These pips have a high acid content which, if mixed with the must, would spoil the wine. Also, the warmth of the soles of the feet assists the early stages of fermentation.

If white wine is being made from black grapes, then the juice must be quickly separated from the skins and stalks, or the wine would be "coloured." Champagne, for example, is largely made from black grapes, and it requires great skill to keep it pure and "white." Red wine, of course, draws its colour from the skins, and the must is usually fermented along with the *râpe*—the skins, stalks and pips.

A natural wine, like claret, is the purest of all beverages. Everything that is required for its production is contained in or on the grape itself. It is only necessary to burst the grape-skin, so that the saccharomycetes can get at the grape-sugar. In the ensuing fermentation, all unwanted bacteria are killed, leaving wine the purest and most hygienic of drinks.

Fermentation

When the grapes have been pressed, and the *cuves*, or vats, cleaned and sterilised, the must is run into them to be fermented. The *cuves* are not filled to the top, to avoid wastage when the must ferments and boils. Usually, however, the minimum necessary amount of air is allowed contact with the must during fermentation. Oxygen encourages the growth of other ferments injurious to the action of the saccharomycetes, and if these were to gain the upper hand, the wine would be spoiled. In some districts, however, no attempt is made to cut off oxygen, and in the fermentation of sherry it is allowed full contact with the must.

Fermentation takes place almost at once, and the liquid bubbles and froths as the carbon-dioxide gas is given off. The first fermentation usually lasts from three days to a week. During this period the temperature of the room must be rigidly stabilised. Within limits, the higher the temperature the easier the fermentation. In more northern districts, therefore, the air is

Many smallholders have their grapes curshed and pressed on the spot

The ancient press of Clos de Vougeot, Burgundy

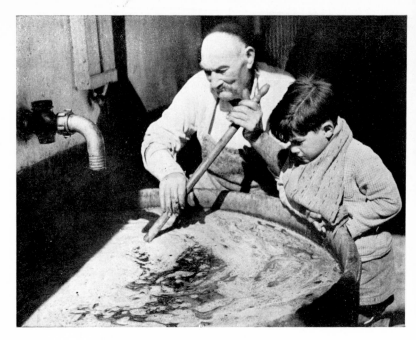

Fermenting must

The wine is repeatedly tested before bottling

artificially warmed to assist fermentation, giving rise to the jibes of the Bordeaux vintners that burgundy tastes of cooked grapes.

The fermentation of port, and other *fortified* wines, is much different from that of natural wines. Port is a wine of high sugar content. If the wine were left to ferment right out, however, nearly all the grape-sugar would be converted into alcohol, and the wine would be dry. The fermentation, therefore, is artificially stopped at an early stage. This is done by the addition to the must of a quantity of alcohol in the form of brandy. The alcoholic content of the must being thus raised, fermentation is cut off and the wine remains rich in sugar.

When the first fermentation of a natural wine is ended, the wine is run off into casks, leaving the *râpe* and sediment behind. The residue of the skins, called *marc*, is mixed with a certain quantity of water, and is used to make poorer-quality wines or spirits. It is necessary to say "first fermentation" because some wines ferment again later, either in cask or in bottle.

The new wine gradually settles in its cask, and throws a sediment, which sinks to the bottom. The wine is then run out into another cask, leaving the unwanted sediment behind. This process, known as "racking," goes on till the wine is quite clear. A final cleansing process, called "fining," is then carried out. A quantity of isinglass or other suitable substance is mixed with the wine. It forms a very fine "net" which, sinking to the bottom, takes down with it the tiniest particles of sediment. The wine is then run off once more, and left to age in wood till bottling time —or till it is shipped abroad.

Wine is a living organism, and, even after bottling, chemical changes are continually taking place. If it is a great wine, it will go on improving for many years. In this process, too, it casts a further sediment. A fine old claret has quite a heavy sediment, while the crust of a vintage port is a well-known phenomenon. It is for this reason that it is necessary to decant old wines and to handle them with the greatest care.

Chapter Three

What is Wine?

WINE is the suitably fermented juice of freshly gathered
grapes, and wine is also a stimulating, wholesome
beverage which has been greatly prized as such among
all the more civilised nations ever since the dawn of history.
There are countless different varieties of wines: wines different
in colour and strength, fragrance and flavour; wines to suit all
men and women, be they rich or not, in health or sickness.

Wines vary, in the first place, according to the very variable
nature of the grape-juice or must from which they are made.
The chemical composition of the must varies according to the
species of vines which produce the grapes; the nature of the soil,
aspect and climate of the vineyards where the vines are grown;
the method of cultivation and the state of the grapes at the time
when they are picked and pressed. Wines vary, in the second
place, according to the manner and degree of fermentation of the
must, and according to the care it receives after fermentation.

Wines may be classed in three main categories: beverage wines;
sparkling wines; fortified wines. Beverage wines, sparkling wines
and fortified wines may be made from any and every kind of
grapes; it is only a matter of letting the must ferment right out
in casks or vats so that the carbon dioxide generated loses itself
in the air (beverage wines), or letting the fermentation take place
partly in bottle so that the generated carbon dioxide is unable to
escape and remains in solution in the wine (sparkling wines), or
checking the fermentation at an early or later stage so that the
wine retains some of its original grape-sugar unfermented (fortified wines).

In each of these three classes there are ever so many different varieties of wines, owing to the differences existing in the chemical composition of the must and the differences in the number and nature of the saccharomycetes present at the vintage or pressing of the grapes. Moreover, although, theoretically, beverage wines, sparkling wines and fortified wines may be made of all and every sort of grape, it is only when made of suitable grapes that they are acceptable.

The bulk of the wines that every year are made throughout the civilised world are beverage wines: black, red, pink, grey, green and golden, mostly common and cheap, and without any particular charm as regards taste and fragrance. They are wholesome, however, because they are free from all germs such as live and thrive in water and milk, and also because they contain a little ethyl alcohol (8 to 12 per cent. by weight), which has a gentle stimulating influence upon the salivary glands and the digestive organs. Such wines are generally at their best when quite young. They usually contain either an excess or a lack of acids which causes them to grow rapidly vapid or sharp with age. But there are other naturally and thoroughly fermented wines which possess in exactly the right proportions the right kinds of acids, sugar and alcohol. They are so well-balanced, so harmoniously built, that the older they are the greater and finer are the volatile ethers which they develop, provided, of course, that they are properly kept and cared for, away from light, air and extremes of heat and cold. Such wines are made only in a few favoured wine-growing districts of the world, where the art of wine-making has been practised for many centuries and has attained to a very high degree of perfection. Of these, the red wines nearly all come from Bordeaux and Burgundy, and the white from the Rhine and Moselle valleys.

Sparkling wines are wines which are rendered sparkling by one of two methods—the wrong one and the right one. The wrong one consists in pumping gas into any wine, and the right one is

to bottle the wine when it still contains sugar which will ferment
and active saccharomycetes which will ensure proper fermentation within the bottle. The carbon dioxide generated by fermentation, being unable to escape, remains in solution in the wine; it
can only escape when the cork is drawn and the wine poured out,
and it is the escape of this carbonic-acid gas in solution in the
wine which causes it to be "bubbly." The presence of carbon
dioxide in a wine may be, and usually is, objectionable; it is only
in the case of the lightest, flimsiest of wines, wines of great
delicacy, that this carbon dioxide is not only acceptable but
greatly desirable. Sparkling wines are made in all wine-producing
countries, but none has ever approached in excellence sparkling
champagne, the prototype.

As all wines may be rendered sparkling, so all may be fortified;
but for this not all are suitable. Generally speaking, the wines
made in Spain, Portugal and Madeira, and also in Australia and
South Africa, possess a greater proportion of natural grape-sugar,
but, when left alone to ferment right out, they lose it all, and
are harsher than wines made in more temperate districts. On the
other hand, these naturally rich-in-sugar wines are the only ones
which are suitable for making fortified wines by the addition of
brandy, which checks fermentation and allows them to retain
some of their original grape-sugar. The finest fortified wine is
port wine, made of a good vintage and matured a sufficiently long
time to attain perfection. Sherry is also a very fine fortified wine,
of which there exist ever so many different varieties, but whilst
the fermentation of port is checked at the time of the vintage,
when the grapes are crushed, sherry is allowed to ferment naturally until it has become wine before brandy is added to it.

A Simple Analysis

Grape-juice, or must, is a very complex aqueous solution,
composed chiefly of water (80 per cent. or more), grape-sugar
(15 per cent. or more), and very minute quantities of a number of

other substances of both vegetable and mineral origin (sulphates, phosphates and other salts); the total amount of these substances never reaches 5 per cent. of the total, and yet their influence upon the quality of the wine is considerable. The two most important parts of must, however, are its grape-sugar and the yeasts, or saccharomycetes, in it.

Grape-sugar is not a compact entity made up of six atoms of carbon, twelve of hydrogen and six of oxygen. There is, it is true, that number of atoms in one molecule of grape-sugar, but they are arranged in two distinct groups—dextrose and fructose. Dextrose and fructose may both be called grape-sugars; their atomic weight is the same, but their molecular grouping is different; and, small as the difference between these two component parts may be, it is important from the point of view of fermentation.

Fermentation consists in a series of complex chemical changes, the most important of which causes the transformation of grape-sugars, i.e. dextrose and fructose, into ethyl alcohol and carbon dioxide. This change is only possible by the catalytic action of a fermenting enzyme known as zymase and when there is a sufficient supply of oxygen. This zymase is supplied by saccharomycetes.

These are generally composed of a single cell, either spherical, elliptical or cylindrical, formed of a thin cell wall containing protoplasm. These cells grow at the expense of other bodies. When the cell of the saccharomycetes reaches a certain size— about ten micro-millimetres—it divides itself into two smaller similar cells, which grow and divide themselves again as soon as they have reached their full size. This process goes on as long as the liquid in which they live supplies to the saccharomycetes sufficient and suitable food; it goes on, however, at a much more rapid rate when the temperature of the liquid is high than when it is low, and it is checked by extremes of heat and cold, by the presence of small quantities of substances such as sulphuric acid, or of too large a proportion of either alcohol or grape-sugar; it is also checked completely by the total absence of oxygen.

The saccharomycetes are the appointed agent of vinous fermentation. Their business is to see that grape-sugar becomes changed into alcohol so that grape-juice may acquire life and become wine. But the saccharomycetes have enemies, other living micro-organisms like themselves: yeasts, moulds and bacteria, millions of which are floating in the air, hanging on cellar walls or cask staves, always ready to pounce upon the grape-juice or wine and start work on their own account. Hence the importance of giving the saccharomycetes every chance, of having as many of them as possible, studying their likes and dislikes in the matter of temperature and surroundings, and being their true allies in the struggle against the power of enemies, chiefly the dreaded moulds.

A wet vintage is always dangerous and often disastrous. A wine made of wet-gathered grapes is never safe, not because of the rain-water in the press, but because of the much smaller number of saccharomycetes upon the grapes, which means that the vinous fermentation will be slow and therefore unsatisfactory.

A suitable temperature for the immediate growth of the saccharomycetes is of great importance, since zymase—their enzyme—is indispensable to alcoholic fermentation. But wine is not merely grape-juice with its grape-sugar changed into alcohol and carbon dioxide; in grape-juice there are many other substances besides grape-sugar, and they cannot be expected to remain unaffected by the internal revolution which destroys the chemical structure of grape-sugar and rebuilds with the same materials ethyl alcohol and carbon dioxide. This revolution is the result of alcoholic fermentation; but other fermentations take place at the same time, other vegetable substances which were in the grape-juice are altered, increased, reduced or may entirely disappear, in ways which differ according to the different enzymes and other catalysts present, as well as according to differences of temperature affecting not only the rate of molecular exchanges, but also the degree of solubility of certain acids.

Water and ethyl alcohol form generally about 97 per cent. of the volume of wine, the remaining 3 per cent. being made up of minute quantities of many other substances which are chiefly responsible for the characteristic individuality of every wine.

These substances may be classed into two categories: those which were present in the must and have undergone no chemical change during fermentation, and those which were not present in the must and may be considered as by-products of fermentation. In the first category are grape-sugar, saccharomycetes, some acids, cellulose, essential oils, etc.; in the second are glycerine, various acids, alcohols other than ethyl alcohol, and volatile esters and aldehydes.

The proportion of grape-sugar that remains in the wine after fermentation depends, in the first place, upon the proportion of grape-sugar present in the must, and, in the second, upon the process or method of fermentation. In the case of "fortified" or "sweet" wines, whether obtained, like port, by the addition of brandy during fermentation, or, like sauternes, from over-ripe grapes, the sweeter the must the sweeter the wine. But in the case of beverage wines, such as claret, it is often the reverse.

The saccharomycetes remain in suspension in the wine until the end of fermentation, or until the proportion of alcohol is such that it arrests their growth. They are so fine and so light that they are neither swept down by finings nor do they fall to the bottom of the cask by their own weight. Many are carried down into the lees by the microscopic crystals of cream of tartar to which they adhere; many more lose their identity altogether by reason of the chemical splitting up of their cells, and some remain in the wine for all time.

Generally speaking, the acids which disappear wholly or partly during fermentation are those which are soluble in water and not in alcohol; whilst acids which appear in much larger proportions in wine than in must are those which are formed by the oxidation of ethyl alcohol.

The principal acid in grape-juice is tartaric acid. It forms a white crystalline salt, commonly known as cream of tartar. Cream of tartar is soluble in water but not in alcohol, and a good deal of the cream of tartar in solution in grape-juice becomes solidified in the shape of white crystals in the presence of the alcohol of wine; in that form it is heavier than wine, settles in the lees, and is left behind when the wine is racked. Cream of tartar is also more soluble in a warm than in a cold solution, so that if a new wine be kept in a cool cellar, the lower temperature, together with the alcohol present, will render a greater proportion of cream of tartar insoluble, thus depriving the wine, after racking, of much acidity present in the must.

But an acid must does not necessarily ferment into an acid wine. Acidity of must is of great benefit, because it assists the normal growth of yeasts and checks the development of bacteria, so that it is favourable to alcoholic fermentation. If as well as acidity there is a fair proportion of grape-sugar in the must, this sugar will ferment and be replaced by a fair proportion of alcohol, which in its turn will cause the crystallisation of a further proportion of cream of tartar, hitherto in solution. In other words, the more sugar in the must means the more alcohol in the wine and the less cream of tartar.

An acid which appears in much larger proportion in wine than in must is acetic acid, formed by the oxidation of ethyl alcohol. The more alcohol there is in a wine, and the less oxygen has access to it, the smaller will be the quantity of acetic acid formed. Again, the chemical change producing it is rendered possible by the presence of an enzyme secreted by the schizomyces, and they cannot grow without a free supply of oxygen from the air. Hence when all contact with the outside air is cut off, no more acetic acid can be formed. On the other hand, wine of a low alcoholic strength, kept in a fairly warm place and in contact with the air, will soon become vinegar, practically the whole of its ethyl alcohol being changed into acetic acid. It should be added, however, that sound wine is seldom free from acetic acid when new, and, with time, this acetic acid dissolves certain mineral salts in wine, forming various acetates which are partly responsible for the flavour and bouquet.

A word, finally, on substances that appear in wine but not in must. They consist chiefly of glycerine and other alcohols, various acids, esters and aldehydes. Pasteur's experiments, which more recent ones have completely confirmed, showed that alcoholic fermentation could not use up more than 95 per cent. of the sugar present in grape-juice, in the proportion of about 48 per cent. ethyl alcohol and 47 per cent. carbon dioxide. The remaining 5 per cent. of sugar is used up in other ways: a small quantity goes to the saccharomycetes themselves by way of food or means of cellular development, a small percentage decomposes into minute quantities of various volatile acids, and the greater proportion is utilised in the production of glycerine. Besides glycerine, which, after and a long way behind ethyl alcohol, is the most important by-product of vinous fermentation, there are other alcohols in wine. Such are propyl and butyl alcohols, and sometimes amyl alcohol. Although these and other alcohols are present in normal wines only in minute quantities, they have, like all alcohols, the property of forming esters with acids, and they play quite an important part, compared to their volume, in the formation of the bouquet or aroma of wine.

First among the acids not contained in the must but appearing in wine is succinic acid, which is the principal cause of the "winy" flavour of wine—its *saveur*. The proportion of succinic acid in a wine, according to Pasteur, is 0.61 per cent. of the grape-sugar in the must. As well as a little acetic acid, there are also small quantities of propionic acid and traces of valerianic acid. These acids do not affect the taste of the wine, but they are responsible to a certain extent for its bouquet. In every case they are present only in minute quantities, but the importance of the part they play upon the degree of excellence of a wine is out of all proportion to their volume.

THE VINEYARDS OF FRANCE

Chapter Four

The Wines of Bordeaux

by Allan Sichel

". . . *To be sold: an entire parcel of New French Claret, being of the growth of Lafitt, Margouze and La Tour. . . .*"—*London Gazette*, 1707.

I

CLARET is often looked upon as a feminine wine. It has been called the Queen of Wines, as opposed to the burgundy King, and in this sense it is perhaps the more feminine. If it is a masculine characteristic of wine that it should test the powers of resistance of the body to alcohol, then again claret is a feminine wine. Without being by any means the least alcoholic of wines, it is, possibly, the least heady. If it is a feminine characteristic to whisper rather than to shout, to be subtle in expression rather than blatant, to reject with age the pleasant flamboyant characteristics of youth in favour of the more tranquil, deeper, more expressive qualities of maturity, then again claret is a feminine wine.

Claret is a kindly, sensitive, proud wine. It will be charming to all who wish to make its acquaintance. It will reveal its innermost self only where confidence will be appreciated and respected. Claret, in short, is capable of expressing beauty and truth, to delight the palate and nurture the mind of the philosopher in all of us. It is food to the mind, not a bludgeon. It reveals its secrets slowly, and becomes at once an inspiration to the striving and a recompense to the successful.

Claret may cost to-day anything from just under one pound a bottle—to several pounds for a rare wine. The cheap wines, offered by reliable wine merchants, represent value that cannot be surpassed by any other wine, and even these, young as they are, and generally the product of a soil a little too rich to produce the refinement of the best growths, are sufficiently versatile and subtle to intrigue the palate during a lifetime of meals. Cheap claret matured in bottle, in its small bin under the stairs or in larger cellars, will develop and improve for five or six years; it can easily become more enjoyable than the immature aristocrats of its region. It offers to all classes of income the same opportunities as are enjoyed by wealthy art connoisseurs and collectors.

Although the finer wines are for special occasions, they should be drunk as opportunity occurs in order that their flavour and bouquet may create in the mind of the beginner a standard against which to measure the lower-priced wines. It is these dearer wines which need a little common-sense selection of accompanying food if all their qualities are to be enjoyed. The rules that matter are few and easily understandable. A strong young claret will go with anything or stand alone. An old, more delicate wine will not generally survive, for example, the strong taste of smoked salmon, will not blend with a fish taste in general, probably not with egg in its cruder forms, or with highly spiced dishes. Beyond this point the question of suitable wines is open to discussion and depends on personal taste. Any poultry, game or meat goes with claret. The regular claret drinker will have no difficulty in finding which particular wine suits various occasions.

II

The modern Gironde, the *département* in which Bordeaux wines are produced, dates from 1790, and is comprised of a part of the old province of Guyenne. It has an area of about four thousand square miles, of which about five hundred square miles are planted with vines. To give an English equivalent, the *département* is about two-thirds the size of Yorkshire, and the vine-yards cover an area about the size of Cambridgeshire. The

Gironde is the largest *département* of France, and is also the largest wine-producing *département*, being responsible for 10 per cent. of all the wine produced in France. More important, it makes about 50 per cent. of all the fine wine of France—that is, of wine entitled under French law to an *Appellation d'Origine Contrôlée*. In a normal year the Gironde produces about eighty-six million gallons of wine, about half of which is white. About two and a half per cent finds its way to the United Kingdom.

Bordeaux itself, a city—half ancient, half modern—of two hundred and seventy thousand inhabitants, is the commercial centre where the great merchant houses have their offices and cellars, and from whose modern port, wines which have matured in the merchant-shippers' cellars are exported all over the world. The city lies mainly on the western bank of the River Garonne. For three miles along its banks stretch the quays where many of the wine houses have their stores and cellars. These Bordeaux cellars, called *chai*, are in reality warehouses rather than cellars: built of massive stone blocks above ground, they cover a large area on the Bordeaux waterfront, and permit of rapid and efficient handling of the thousands of casks that are yearly rolled in and out of their high wooden doors.

Along the banks of the Gironde and the Garonne, for some forty miles to the north of Bordeaux and thirty miles to the south, stretch the vineyard areas, while to the east of the city, and on the other side of the river, they extend to a depth of twenty-five miles within the same north and south limits.

The Garonne, which flows roughly north-westerly from its source in the Pyrénées, is joined about ten miles north of Bordeaux by the swift-flowing Dordogne on its course from the central plateau of France. They meet to form the Gironde.

The countryside is in part disappointing to the visitor. The western side of the river forms very gently undulating country to the north of Bordeaux; to the south, only slightly more hilly. The roads, hedgeless and often dusty, are bordered by pleasing stretches of vineyard, occasional clumps of fir-trees, and occasional shabby and untidy villages. They rarely offer an extensive view. The main road southwards towards Biarritz and Spain is well made; there are fewer villages along its length, and the hilly country across the river offers a more picturesque landscape. The climate from May to October is generally fine, and in mid-summer and August is very hot. Otherwise, it is damp and similar in many ways to a mild English winter.

III

Bordeaux has produced wines since the dawn of its history. The first reports of its wines date from the Roman occupation, but it was several centuries later, when the marriage of Eleanor of Aquitaine (the ancient name for Guyenne) to Henry II of England brought the whole of the province of Guyenne, including Gascony, into the possession of the English kings, that the wines of the country became known in England. Neither vineyards nor wines, however, were as we know them to-day. At least three hundred years were to elapse before the first cork was used, and about five hundred before wine was put into glass bottles.

The vineyards in those early days were no more than strips of vines in the cornfields, small patches, mostly in the area just to the south of Bordeaux. The wine they produced was light in colour, often made of a mixture of red and white grapes, and was drunk young—within a year of being made. It was, at that time, a crime to sell old wine as new. The merchants of the Sénéchaussée of Bordeaux enjoyed the sole rights of selling wine from the Feast of St. Martin until Easter. The wine was lighter in colour than that from the southern vineyards, and it is believed that the designation *Clairet*, by which it was known, is the origin of the word *claret* used to-day.

Nowadays the products of the Bordeaux vineyards are esteemed mainly because of their ability to develop in bottle such delicacy of flavour and aroma that not only is the resultant character

The grapes are cut by hand, and the pickers come from all over the country for the harvest

Château Latour

Loading grapes in the Lafite vineyard

intrinsically pleasing but also pleasantly intriguing. Not only does it become possible to recognise a particular wine as a personality, but it becomes impossible to analyse that personality, so perfect is the harmony of the component flavours.

The soil on which the vines are grown is poor soil, suitable for no other crops. The vines themselves have, through the centuries, been selected and developed until to-day each type of soil is planted with the vine that suits it best, each estate has arrived at just the right proportion of the various authorised vines to suit its local climate. The poor soil contains no excess of any one substance; the vine is not too greedy for any single form of nourishment. The wine itself is made with no interference from man; every minute degree of substance in the soil plays its part, unhampered by any excess of sugar or alcohol, in creating such a rhythm and harmony in the resultant wine that a light Bordeaux of a perfect year may live and improve for half a century.

The white wines of Bordeaux have achieved their own fame on their merits and by the variety of types produced. The light, dry wines, obtainable at reasonably low prices by to-day's standards, are refreshing and nourishing; while the finest and most voluptuous *Sauternes* can give a sensation of warmth, maturity and well-being to the palate which nothing can emulate.

It is generally considered that the wines of Bordeaux fall into five main groups—three red and two white. The three red are known by the name of the viticultural areas of *Médoc*, *Graves* and *St. Émilion*; the white by *Graves* and *Sauternes*. There are, however, other districts which account for a substantial amount of the wines exported, and their existence must therefore be recorded. They appear in the table following the chapter.

The nomenclature of Bordeaux wines is simple, and yet is widely misunderstood. It is clear that of the many permanent factors influencing the character of a wine, there are two that are paramount—the soil and the vine. Of these, the soil alone is suitable as a characteristic for grouping types of wine, and therefore the Gironde or Bordeaux area is divided into various *viti-cultural districts* according to the general nature of the soil on which the vines are grown. These districts are further subdivided into *communes*, which are the villages or parishes as administered under local government laws. Within these parish boundaries there exist various estates—called *châteaux*, *domaines* or *clos*—owning vineyards, sometimes in one area only, sometimes in separate localities. The best of these estates give their own name to the wines, the small peasant holdings being content, generally, for their wine to be known by the name of the commune, since they are not of a quality to make them recognisable as individuals.

As a further subdivision of the estates, there exists an official classification according to *quality* for the red wines of the *Médoc* and for the white wines of *Sauternes*. The classification was made in 1855. In 1953 the wines of St. Émilion were officially classified into two groups, Premier Grand Cru Classé—naming twelve wines—and Grand Cru Classé—naming sixty wines. Unlike the Médoc classification, the St. Émilion list must be confirmed by the proper authorities at specified intervals. The wines of the 1855 classification are known as *classed growths*; for red wines there are sixty-two estates classified into five groups, the highest being the 1st Classed Growths, the lowest the 5th Classed Growths. In addition to these, there are about 3,000 estates classified as Bourgeois Supérieur, Bourgeois and Artisan growths. These, however, do not generally carry their classification on the label, and are known as Bourgeois Growths as opposed to Classed Growths.

In the classification of the white wines there are only twenty-two estates listed, divided into two classes, with one, the Château d'Yquem, classed by itself as a *Premier Grand Cru*. In addition to these, however, there are something under two hundred other estates of repute in the Sauternes region.

It will be noticed that in the table at the end of the chapter the name *Sauternes* appears twice—first as a viticultural area and secondly as a parish or commune. This is because the name of the

BORDEAUX

most famous commune—in which the renowned Château d'Yquem is situated—is used to designate the whole viticultural area. In practice, the only parish name invariably used is that of *Barsac*, most of the châteaux in other parishes contenting themselves with the use of the area name of Sauternes. The Classed growths, however, usually indicate on their labels the parish in which they are situated.

Under a special "Statute Vinicole," the law of France provides for the control of the descriptions of wines. These laws lay down certain conditions which are supposed to be fulfilled by the grower who wishes to use the name of his parish or viticultural area. He must, for example, grow his vines within a prescribed area, plant only specified vines and not exceed a specified number of vines per acre. He must not produce a quantity of wine in excess of a specified maximum per acre. There is also a minimum sugar content which the pressed juice must contain and a minimum alcoholic content which the finished wine must attain. There are also regulations governing the planting and pruning of the vines. These regulations are known as the law *d'Appellation d'Origine Contrôlée*, and are largely effective in preventing malpractices.

IV

Wine-making in the Gironde

The character and health-giving qualities of Bordeaux wines are largely due to the method of wine-making employed. In all essentials it is still the natural and unhampered method by which wine has always been made. Bordeaux is favoured with a climate and soil pre-eminently suited for the making of wine. It is not surprising, therefore, that in the course of time the Bordelais have initiated laws which govern the other two main factors in the production of fine wine—the type of vine planted and the method of making the wine.

There are six varieties of plants authorised: the Cabernet, the Cabernet Sauvignon, the Merlot, the Petit Verdot, the Malbec and the Carmenère. With slight variations in different districts, these are the only vines that can be used for the production of red wines entitled to an *Appellation Contrôlée*. They are known under different names in the different districts. In St. Émilion, for example, the Cabernet and Malbec are known as the Bouchet and Pressac, but the plants are identical.

There are four vines authorised for the making of white wines —two main plants, the Sémillon and Sauvignon, with the subsidiary Muscadelle for the sweet wine districts, and an additional subsidiary for Graves, the Muscadet.

The vine flowers generally during the first ten days of June, and the grape is ready for picking one hundred days later—in the event of the weather having been normal. Fine, warm weather is needed during the flowering. Cold, wet, changeable weather will prevent setting of the fruit, and a grower may well be faced with the loss of half his crop three or four months before the vintage. This does not mean that he can stint the care of his vineyard for the rest of that year. He knows he must lose money that year, but he knows also that to reduce the loss to a minimum he must not skimp the expense or trouble involved in the care of his vines.

The vine is subject to many diseases. The scourge of *Phylloxera*, which decimated the vineyards in the 1880s, first reached Bordeaux in 1869. Slowly the insect gnawed away the roots of the vines. The *Phylloxera* came from America, and so, eventually, did the cure, in the shape of American vine stocks immune from the louse. The old French vines were grafted on to these stocks, and this scourge, at least, is almost unknown to-day, and the quality of the wines is generally considered not to have suffered. Other scourges, however, appear regularly, and the days and purse of the *vigneron* are spent in preventive measures: copper sulphate is sprayed at regular intervals to combat the *mildew* which first appeared about 1878; sulphur is sprayed to counteract *oidium*, a parasitic fungus, which was first noticed as early as 1834, and which played havoc with the vineyards for nearly twenty years until the cure was found. The worse the climatic conditions in any year, the greater the need and the greater the number of these expensive treatments. It costs more to produce a bad wine than a good wine.

Generally speaking, each proprietor in the Gironde makes his own wine, although amongst the smaller peasant proprietors the co-operative movement is spreading. In the red wine districts, the grapes are gathered about the middle of September. This is an anxious period for the proprietor. He must take the decision when to gather the berries. The weather may be wet, the grape over-ripe from a hot summer. Shall he wait for sun to-morrow or the day after, and risk losing his crop if there is no sun, or shall he gather what he has and risk making a wine poorer than that of his neighbours who decide to wait? Depending upon the size of his property, the gathering may take a few days, or three weeks, and the proprietor has to arrange for the labour—troupes of vintagers organised rather on the lines of the hop-pickers in England. Whether they are working or not, he must house and feed them. So there are always a myriad technical considerations influencing the decision.

In the red wine districts the grapes are gathered all at once by the bunch; in the case of white wines the vineyard may have to be gone through several times, only the ripest grapes being picked each time. Sometimes, in the Sauternes district, one grape at a time is picked, because here the "noble rot," or *pourriture noble* of the grapes, is essential to the making of a fine wine. This "noble rot" manifests itself as a white mould on the skin of the grape at a time when the berry is shrivelled by the heat of the sun; it is primarily responsible for the characteristic unctuous flavour of the fine white wines. It may take a hundred and fifty men days to pick sufficient grapes to make one cask of wine.

The red grapes, when gathered, are taken to the *cuvier*—the vat-room—of the proprietor. There the grapes, with or without stalks, are lightly pressed, by foot or by machine, and pumped into large vats—stalks, skins and juice together in many cases, depending upon the wine being made. The must then ferments for five or six days, while the saccharomycetes turn the grape-sugar into alcohol, and the colour is drawn from the skins into the wine. The process of fermentation is a complicated, natural procedure. Owing, however, to the researches of the great Pasteur in the 1850s, it is now well understood. The newly fermented wine is then drawn off the large vats, which hold forty or fifty hogsheads each, into small hogshead casks holding forty-eight gallons each. This is done about a week after fermentation starts, or as soon as labour is obtainable from the vineyards where the gathering is still in progress.

In the white wine areas, particularly in that of Sauternes, the fermentation takes place in hogsheads which have to be filled up every day, as the fermentation reduces the bulk and spills wine through the bunghole by its force. In this case, only the juice is pumped into the casks to ferment. The white grape skins are not required, but are pressed again in an electric, hydraulic, or hand-press to produce the *vin de presse*, which may or may not be added to the first wine, according to its quality or to the policy of the owner.

After Nature has produced the grape, much depends on the care, the courage and the honesty of man. There are good wines which are ruined by the "improvements" man tries to make, and there are good potential wines ruined by his carelessness or ignorance.

At least two, and sometimes three, years of care and treatment have to be given to the wines from the time they are first made and drawn off their lees into the hogsheads, before they begin, properly, to become Bordeaux. The process of development is long and regular. The newly fermented wine contains many impurities which will spoil its taste: excesses of this or that particular constituent part. For example, it has at the beginning a small residue of sugar which will gradually ferment during the first year, but in the case of fine white wines may require some-times two or even three years. These changes are largely due to living organic organisms, and during their operation the living Bordeaux is as subject to the influence of unhealthy organisms as are human beings.

Whilst still in its young state, the wine is often bought by one or more of the leading shipping houses of Bordeaux. The shippers do not, of course, own their own ships—though throughout the summer they are constantly being asked by enthusiastic young wine students whether a passage can be had to Bordeaux! They train and prepare the young wine for its journey abroad, and are responsible for ensuring that each wine goes to the type of home for which it is most suited. Treatment consists of no more than helping Nature develop the wine by assuring that it is kept at the proper cool temperature, by racking it off the lees, or deposit, at the bottom of the cask whenever necessary, by assisting the process of clarification, if required, by fining, and by making sure that the wine is not released for bottling until its organic develop-ment has reached its peak. It is then ready for the gentle chemical changes which are brought about in the bottle, and which produce the aroma, the velvety softness and the infinity of fleeting flavours which are characteristic of a fine Bordeaux wine naturally pro-duced and competently nursed.

The majority of wines are shipped from Bordeaux in wood and bottled by wine merchants in Great Britain. At the present rate of duty this saves the consumer about five shillings a bottle, partly because of duty but also because of freight charges and "château bottling" costs. The standard of bottling in the United Kingdom is very high, and is certainly not surpassed in any other country. There are also students of wine who maintain that a Bordeaux, shipped in wood and allowed a few weeks to breathe the atmosphere of its new home, eventually makes a better bottle than one bottled on its own native soil. There is at least one classic example of this on the market in Britain to-day.

Château Margaux

"On adore son nom aux deux bouts de la terre . . ."

" Boy Drinking"
by
Murillo

French Glass : A fine 17th-century glass similar to the one in the painting by
Murillo

A modern "cuvier" in the Gironde

A vat of wine

Some famous châteaux ship their wine "château bottled," and these bear on their label the words "*Mise en bouteilles au château*" or "*Mise du château*," or similar phrase. There is one famous château that *never* "château bottles." "Château-bottling" guarantees exactly what it says, that the wine was bottled by the château. It does not guarantee, except by somewhat illogical inference, that it is a *good* wine that was bottled at the château. The only satisfactory guarantee of this is the assurance, not of a poor and perhaps harassed proprietor who has to sell what Nature has given him, but the recommendation of a reputable wine merchant who selected the wine out of many offered to him and whose most valuable asset is his own reputation.

Wherever the wine is bottled, it will be well looked after, kept in a cool, dark cellar where it can lie undisturbed until ready for drinking, or for transfer to an empty bin-case in the cupboard under the stairs or in the cellars of clubs, hotels or of the wealthy. Bordeaux may be ready to drink two or twenty years after bottling. As it ages, it gradually loses its deep colour, casts as a dry deposit any excess tannin, develops a bouquet through the action of its lighter alcohols, the extent and variety of which, happily enough, no chemist can measure or even explain. In time it will be as good as it can be, and generally thereafter it will slowly decline until, over a period of years, it gracefully fades away altogether. The 1870 Lafite did not mature until the fifties, the 1960 is past its best. Such are the possibilities of variation. Only the wine merchant can advise the consumer, and he only if his customer will take the trouble to consult him and tell him exactly what he is looking for.

v

The Red Wine Areas of Bordeaux

The most famous and most important wine-producing area of Bordeaux is the *Médoc*, which, to the west of the Garonne and Gironde, stretches north from Bordeaux for over forty miles, and has an average depth of over six miles. It is divided into two parts, the southern three-quarters of its length being known as Haut-Médoc, and containing all the best wine areas, whilst the Bas-Médoc makes wines of lesser calibre. The soil is largely gravel mixed with sand and earth, and sometimes limestone. It varies a good deal throughout the area, some districts having a thick layer of heavy, clay-like soil. The country is uninteresting, giving a uniform impression of flatness, although it is really a plateau well above the river level. In general, the southern parishes of *Macau*, *Ludon*, *Margaux*, *Moulis*, *Listrac*, *Cantenac*, *Arsac* and *Labarde* produce lighter wines than those to the north, such as *St. Julien*, *Pauillac* and *St. Estèphe*.

Château Margaux, which produces one of the most famous of the First Growths, is one of the oldest estates of the Médoc, with a history dating back to the fifteenth century, when it was called Château de Lamothe. It was of Margaux that the poet wrote:

> "*On adore son nom aux deux bouts de la terre;*
> *De ce château divin tout peuple est tributaire . . .*
> *Quand des rois d'aujourd'hui la puissance chancelle,*
> *La sienne grandit seule; elle est seule immortelle.*"

The other two First Growths of the Médoc—Château Lafite and Château Latour—are at Pauillac, as is also Château Mouton-Rothschild, which for many years now has ranked with the First Growths, and often fetches a higher price than these.

Clarets like these are surely the greatest wines in the world. Although they may have less "body" than a fine Burgundy, they have a finesse, a delicacy, that is unrivalled by any other wines. Their colour alone is a joy—no trace of purple, but a pure, clear, deep ruby. Their enjoyment is not that of the palate alone, but of the senses of sight and smell every bit as much.

The homes of the other classed growths of the Médoc can be seen from the list at the end. These wines, right down to the Fifth Growths, are great wines—always provided that they are of a good year. The estates vary greatly in size, some of the biggest, such as Château Pontet Canet at Pauillac, making as much as eight hundred hogsheads a year. Four hundred hogsheads is not an unusual crop amongst the classed growths; few make less than one hundred. Amongst the Bourgeois and Artisan classes there are innumerable small properties making only twenty to thirty casks a year.

The district of *Graves* (*Red Graves*)—the same area as the White Graves—contains many properties. It stretches for about thirty miles south of Bordeaux, with an average depth westwards from the river towards the sea of about ten miles. The soil, as the name implies, is largely made up of a stony, sandy mixture of varying depth, with a limestone or clay-mixed subsoil. The wines are often remarkable for their brilliant colour, and have a well-defined taste and aroma different from those of the Médoc.

The most famous of all the estates is the Château Haut-Brion, the only wine in this area classified in the Official Classification of 1855. It is a First Classed Growth. The district of Pessac, in which the château is situated, is contiguous with the city boundary, and contains many other famous properties, such as the Pape-Clément —recently reconstituted—and La Mission Haut-Brion, an entirely separate property. South of Pessac, in the parish of Léognan, are the Château Haut-Bailly, the Domaine de Chevalier, the Château Carbonnieux and many others. More fine red wine than white is made in this area. These two parishes, with that of Villenave d'Ornon and the land upon which part of the city of Bordeaux now stands, are the original home of the *Clairet* wines first shipped to England in the twelfth century. The parish of Martillac, in which are the vineyards of Château Smith-Haut-Lafite, also produces more red than white wine.

The red wines of Graves live long in bottle, and develop a refined quality which is much sought after. There are some thirty-five parishes in the Graves area, but most of the fine red wine is produced in the few named above.

VI

About twenty miles east of Bordeaux, across the Garonne, across the plateau of the Entre-Deux-Mers and across the Dordogne, to the east of Libourne, lies the comparatively small area of *St. Émilion*. It covers perhaps forty or fifty square miles of fairly hilly country, closely packed with vineyards and crisscrossed by narrow, dusty, hedgeless country roads.

The town of St. Émilion is picturesque in the extreme, and dominates from its hill the ten square miles—6,500 acres—of vineyards clustered on the hill-side around it. The soil is here largely a mixture of clay and limestone, with sometimes a strong admixture of stone. The subsoil is, in general, gravelly. The whole composition is almost the reverse of the Médoc. The wines are big and generous, with less finesse than those of the Médoc, but with more body.

Here the vine is often pruned higher, and may stand three feet from the ground. In hot years, like 1921, when the lower-growing grapes of the Médoc may suffer from lack of moisture and pitiless radiation of heat from the pebbly soil on the unprotected underside of the grapes, the wines of St. Émilion, growing a little higher, and benefiting from moisture retained in the heavier soil, sometimes produce such magnificent wines as the Château Cheval-Blanc 1921. This property, whose vines grow on a ridge known as the *Graves de St. Émilion*, and Château Ausone, just outside the borders of the town itself, are the two most renowned of the St. Émilion estates. Ausone has very picturesque cellars dug out of the limestone rock below the vineyard. There are twelve wines in all, including the above, classified officially as Premier Grand Cru Classé St. Émilion, and a further sixty classified as Grand Cru Classé St. Émilion; in addition there are some one hundred further estates whose wines are entitled to be described as St. Émilion and who, with a host of smaller proprietors, must submit their wines each year for official approval.

Abutting on the true St. Émilion area are six small areas not entitled to call their wines St. Émilion, but known as *Lussac-St. Émilion*, *Montagne-St. Émilion*, *Parsac-St. Émilion*, *Puisseguin-St. Émilion*, *St. Georges-St. Émilion* and *Sables-St. Émilion*.

The districts of *Pomerol*, *Néac* and *Lalande de Pomerol* cover together an area roughly three-quarters that of St. Émilion, and form a continuation of that district to the north-west. The soil is sandier, has a larger proportion of pebbles than St. Émilion, but has the same clay, iron-rich subsoil. The wines have a finer bouquet, and are, in a way, more austere, without being at all hard. There are between 170 and 180 principal growths, the most famous of which are often seen in Britain, and all of which are accepted as Pomerol First Growths.

A few miles west of Pomerol, and a couple of miles north-west of Libourne, lies the very small area of *Fronsac*, since 1939 divided into the *Côtes de Fronsac* and the *Côtes de Canon Fronsac*. The country is picturesque, and there are some good wines made, but the soil is here beginning to be too rich, and the wines, pleasing, soft and round as they are, lack the distinction of the Pomerols and St. Émilions.

Well to the north of Fronsac, and about twelve miles down the river, on the east bank of the Gironde below the confluence of the Garonne and Dordogne, lie the fairly large wine areas of *Bourg* and *Blaye*. They form one of the most picturesque areas of the Gironde. The soil is rich and the wines are generous. There is a multitude of small wines, good and satisfying when two or three years old, but few of any individuality or more than local reputation. The better wines of each district are known as Côtes de Bourg and Côtes de Blaye.

Finally, to the east of the Garonne, opposite the Graves district, are the *Premières Côtes de Bordeaux*, formed of low hills bordering the river, and stretching for some twenty-five miles, with a depth of not more than a mile or two. The wines are pleasant without great distinction. This area is the home of the

Clairet of to-day—a light pink wine that makes a good cold thirst-quencher on a hot day.

VII

The White Wine Areas of Bordeaux

White wines are made in two main areas—those of Graves and Sauternes. They are made also in the Entre-Deux-Mers, in the Blayais, and, opposite the Sauternes area, in the two small districts of Ste.-Croix-du-Mont and Loupiac, on the east bank of the Garonne.

The *Blayais*, as already mentioned, makes with Bourg good useful red wines from its rich soil. It produces, however, far more white wine than red—unlike Bourg which makes more red than white. It is an area of large production and in practice makes over twice as much wine to the acre as the Sauternes district. The wines are light in alcohol, of ordinary quality and not generally exported. They are known as Blaye, Côte de Blaye and Première Côte de Blaye, according to their quality.

The vast area of *Entre-Deux-Mers*, forty miles long and ten broad, is richly planted with vines, and produces about 10 per cent. of all the wine in the Bordeaux area. The name is reserved for the white wines of the area, for which the authorised production is higher even than that of Blayais. There is a considerable variation in soil over the area, but in general the wines suitable for export come from vines planted in the sandy-clay soil of the higher ground rather than in the rich alluvial soil of the marshy low levels. There are a very large number of parishes in the area, none of which are *Appellations Contrôlées*.

Within the area of Entre-Deux-Mers, almost opposite Libourne on the banks of the Dordogne, is the small area of *Graves de Vayres*, so called because of its "Graves" soil. Although its wines are somewhat above the Entre-Deux-Mers quality, it should not be confused with the product of Graves proper. The *Premières Côtes de Bordeaux*, mentioned under the red wine areas, is also geographically part of the Entre-Deux-Mers. Although it is predominantly a red wine area, it includes several good white wine areas, such as *Verdelais*, *Gabarnac*, *Monprimblanc*, *Donzac*, *Cadillac*, *Rions*, *Langoiran* and *Tabanac*. There is much good wine-growing soil here, and wines from this area are well worth consideration.

Two famous areas enclosed, in their turn, within the boundaries of the *Premières Côtes*, exactly opposite *Sauternes* on the east bank of the Garonne, are *Loupiac* and *Sainte-Croix-du-Mont*. They are entitled to their own appellations. The wines of the two districts are quite different in character. The Ste.-Croix-du-Mont's are generally light in colour, with a greenish tinge, and are like the Barsacs in taste, while the Loupiacs are often deeper and more yellow in colour and resemble the more seductive Sauternes. Both areas have a clay-limestone soil, but Ste.-Croix-du-Mont has a stonier subsoil than Loupiac, which has a good deal of clay.

The only wine actually named after the soil on which its famous wines grow is that of *Graves*. It will be remembered that it contains about thirty-five parishes. A large number of these produce good white wine. It is the custom to think of these wines as "dry," but in fact there is great variety in their degree of sweetness. In general, the finest wines are the driest—wine such as the white Domaine de Chevalier (now producing scarcely any white wine since the vineyard was destroyed by a hailstorm a few years ago), the Château Carbonnieux, Château le Pape (not to be confused with the Pape-Clément at Pessac which makes red wine only), all at Léognan, and Château Couhins at Villenave d'Ornon. These are amongst the finest White Graves and all are dry.

Recently six Graves wines have been classified as Graves Cru Classé. They will be found on page 75. In addition to these, there is a large number of vineyards producing differing styles and qualities of wine. Production per acre is much greater than in the Sauternes, and good wines, which develop greatly in bottle, are made throughout the whole area, and are available at very reasonable prices in Great Britain or America.

The area of *Cérons*, although only four miles by six, includes not only the parish of Cérons, but those of Podensac and Illats as well. Geographically, it forms a link between Graves and Sauternes, and its wines, in quality and character, are also a link between the areas. The soil is gravel, with a stony subsoil; there is little clay, and the resultant wines are of great delicacy and finely made. Cérons is one of the most recently recognised viticultural areas, and includes vineyards formerly looked upon as either Graves or Sauternes.

Sauternes is the most famous of all French white wine districts. It covers an area of about forty square miles, and contains five communes within its boundaries, all of great repute: Sauternes, Barsac, Bommes, Fargues and Preignac. Of these, *Barsac* is entitled to its own appellation, and its wines are generally known by its name. The soil at Barsac is a mixture of limestone and clay on a limestone subsoil, while the rest of the area is predominantly gravel on a clay subsoil. The characteristic Barsac is different in flavour from the rest of the Sauternes wines. It is generally green-tinged in colour, and has a more austere form than the wines of the other parishes, whilst retaining to the full the softness and beauty of their flavour. This richness of flavour, which comes from the special methods of vinification practised in the area, is the outstanding characteristic of all the wines of Sauternes. The over-ripeness of the grape is reflected in the remarkable flavour of the wine. Paramount among the other Sauternes, of course, is the great Château d'Yquem—in a class by itself.

Pressing the grapes into a bucket before taking them to the château

Château d'Yquem

The cellar-master, Château d'Yquem

VIII

The Serving of Claret

Claret does not form a crust as does vintage port, and to that extent its handling is easier. It can be transferred from a merchant's to a private cellar at any stage of its development, provided it is given a few weeks' rest to get over the tiring effect of the journey—if it happens to be an old gentleman. The younger the wine, the more robust it is, the less deposit it has to become unsettled, and the shorter the rest it requires.

The bottle must always be stored lying down, so that the cork is in contact with the wine, and is thus kept moist. It should be stored in a cool place—in practice this means up to 60° F. and not below 45° or so, if it is to be kept for several years. If the wine is to be drunk within a year, it will develop between the limits of 40° and 65° F.

There is no mystery about the serving and decanting of wine. In the first place, a good bottle of claret can be enjoyed at any time, with or without a meal. It is currently drunk in France with fish. Strongly flavoured dishes such as smoked salmon, curry or fried eggs may not give a fine red wine much chance to show its finesse—but, after all, some people like to bath in champagne or to drink it out of slippers! Wine is a joyous gift of Providence, and should be used as such. The majority will wish to obtain the greatest pleasure out of their wine, and will drink the more delicate old bottles only with food which does not kill its flavour.

Decanting is resorted to for one main reason—to pour the clear wine off the deposit which it has probably, but not necessarily, thrown off during its development. Therefore, if the wine is wanted for the table within a few hours, and if it has a deposit, it should be decanted. Obviously, it should be quietly taken, in its lying down position, and placed in a decanting basket, or anywhere else where it can be uncorked without being shaken, twisted or turned. Some sort of lever-action or double-screw-action corkscrew is essential, to avoid the explosive jerk as the cork comes out. The wine is then gently poured into a decanter or clean bottle over the light of a candle or electric torch, which, seen through the shoulder or neck of the horizontal bottle, will show up quite clearly any deposit moving towards the lip. When the deposit reaches the lip, one stops decanting, stands up the bottle, and uses the cloudy wine in the kitchen for sauces.

Before starting to pour, the lip of the bottle should be cleaned with a clean cloth, and the decanter should be clean and not ice-cold.

If there is no deposit, it is not necessary to decant, and, even if there is, if twenty-four hours' notice is available, it is not necessary to use a decanting basket, since the bottle can be very gently stood up so that the deposit slides to the bottom and is to some extent trapped in the punt. This, in fact, is the preferable method, since the act of standing the bottle upright seems to give it an opportunity to "stretch its legs," as it were, and to release its flavour and aroma in a more lively manner when it is opened a day later.

Glasses should be shaped so that the aroma is concentrated at the lip; they should be big enough to hold a reasonable amount of wine when two-thirds filled. They should never be filled higher than this or the aroma may be lost.

There are too many exceptions to make it possible to recommend vintages. So-called bad vintages nearly always produce some good wine, which, in view of its low reputation, is generally obtainable at a very favourable price. Conversely, *bad* wines are made in good years—and bad wine is expensive at any price. Only the recommendations of a good wine merchant can assure the guidance necessary in buying any wine. Choose your wine merchant with care—then trust him or leave him.

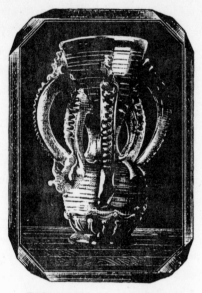

THE WINES OF BORDEAUX
A SHORT LIST

BO

(Showing Viticultural Distri

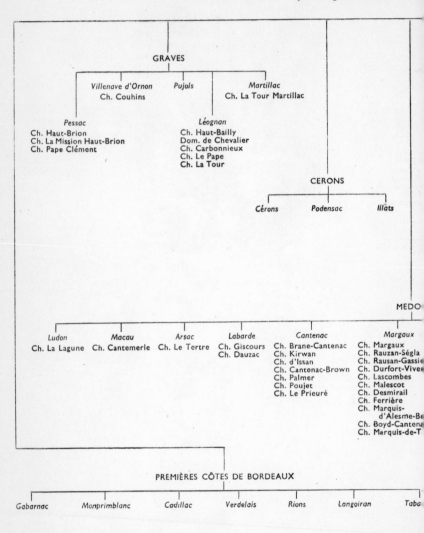

GRAVES

Villenave d'Ornon   Pujols   Martillac
Ch. Couhins   Ch. La Tour Martillac

Pessac   Léognan
Ch. Haut-Brion   Ch. Haut-Bailly
Ch. La Mission Haut-Brion Dom. de Chevalier
Ch. Pape Clément   Ch. Carbonnieux
                          Ch. Le Pape
                          Ch. La Tour

CERONS

Cérons   Podensac   Illats

MEDO

Ludon   Macau   Arsac   Labarde   Cantenac   Margaux
Ch. La Lagune Ch. Cantemerle Ch. Le Tertre Ch. Giscours Ch. Brane-Cantenac Ch. Margaux
                                         Ch. Dauzac   Ch. Kirwan   Ch. Rauzan-Ségla
                                                      Ch. d'Issan   Ch. Rausan-Gassie
                                                      Ch. Cantenac-Brown Ch. Durfort-Vive
                                                      Ch. Palmer   Ch. Lascombes
                                                      Ch. Poujet   Ch. Malescot
                                                      Ch. Le Prieuré   Ch. Desmirail
                                                                        Ch. Ferrière
                                                                        Ch. Marquis-
                                                                            d'Alesme-Be
                                                                        Ch. Boyd-Cantena
                                                                        Ch. Marquis-de-T

PREMIÈRES CÔTES DE BORDEAUX

Gabarnac   Monprimblanc   Cadillac   Verdelais   Rions   Langoiran   Taba

68

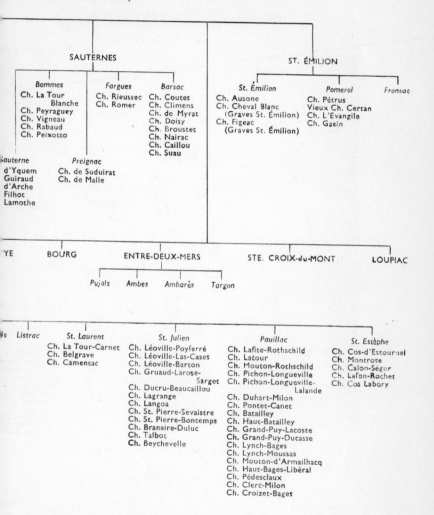

SAUTERNES — ST. ÉMILION

Bommes
Ch. La Tour
    Blanche
Ch. Peyraguey
Ch. Vigneau
Ch. Rabaud
Ch. Peixotto

Fargues
Ch. Rieussec
Ch. Romer

Barsac
Ch. Coutet
Ch. Climens
Ch. de Myrat
Ch. Doisy
Ch. Broustet
Ch. Nairac
Ch. Caillou
Ch. Suau

St. Émilion
Ch. Ausone
Ch. Cheval Blanc
  (Graves St. Émilion)
Ch. Figeac
  (Graves St. Émilion)

Pomerol
Ch. Pétrus
Vieux Ch. Certan
Ch. L'Evangile
Ch. Gazin

Fronsac

Sauterne
d'Yquem
Guiraud
d'Arche
Filhot
Lamothe

Preignac
Ch. de Suduirat
Ch. de Malle

YE   BOURG   ENTRE-DEUX-MERS   STE. CROIX-du-MONT   LOUPIAC

Pujols   Ambes   Ambarès   Targon

...is   Listrac

St. Laurent
Ch. La Tour-Carnet
Ch. Belgrave
Ch. Camensac

St. Julien
Ch. Léoville-Poyferré
Ch. Léoville-Las-Cases
Ch. Léoville-Barton
Ch. Gruaud-Larose-
           Sarget
Ch. Ducru-Beaucaillou
Ch. Lagrange
Ch. Langoa
Ch. St. Pierre-Sevaistre
Ch. St. Pierre-Bontemps
Ch. Branaire-Duluc
Ch. Talbot
Ch. Beychevelle

Pauillac
Ch. Lafite-Rothschild
Ch. Latour
Ch. Mouton-Rothschild
Ch. Pichon-Longueville
Ch. Pichon-Longueville-
           Lalande
Ch. Duhart-Milon
Ch. Pontet-Canet
Ch. Batailley
Ch. Haut-Batailley
Ch. Grand-Puy-Lacoste
Ch. Grand-Puy-Ducasse
Ch. Lynch-Bages
Ch. Lynch-Moussas
Ch. Mouton-d'Armailhacq
Ch. Haut-Bages-Libéral
Ch. Pédesclaux
Ch. Clerc-Milon
Ch. Croizet-Bages

St. Estèphe
Ch. Cos-d'Estournel
Ch. Montrose
Ch. Calon-Ségur
Ch. Lafon-Rochet
Ch. Cos Labory

THE WINES OF BORDEAUX

Red Wines

1. Médoc

The great classification of the red wines of the Médoc was made in 1855. Since then, some châteaux have been split into two parts, others have slightly altered or added to their names. The following list preserves the original classification, but incorporates later additions and changes:

First Growths

Château	*Commune*
LAFITE-ROTHSCHILD	PAUILLAC
MARGAUX	MARGAUX
LATOUR	PAUILLAC
HAUT-BRION (GRAVES)	PESSAC (GRAVES)

Second Growths

MOUTON-ROTHSCHILD	PAUILLAC
RAUSAN-SÉGLA	MARGAUX
RAUZAN-GASSIES	MARGAUX
LÉOVILLE-LAS-CASES	ST. JULIEN
LÉOVILLE-POYFERRÉ	ST. JULIEN
LÉOVILLE-BARTON	ST. JULIEN
DURFORT-VIVENS	MARGAUX
LASCOMBES	MARGAUX
GRUAUD-LAROSE	ST. JULIEN
BRANE-CANTENAC	CANTENAC
PICHON-LONGUEVILLE	PAUILLAC
PICHON-LONGUEVILLE-LALANDE	PAUILLAC
DUCRU-BEAUCAILLOU	ST. JULIEN
COS-D'ESTOURNEL	ST. ESTÈPHE
MONTROSE	ST. ESTÈPHE

Third Growths

KIRWAN	CANTENAC
D'ISSAN	CANTENAC
LAGRANGE	ST. JULIEN
LANGOA (BARTON)	ST. JULIEN
GISCOURS	LABARDE
MALESCOT-SAINT-EXUPÉRY	MARGAUX
CANTENAC-BROWN	CANTENAC

Château	*Commune*
PALMER	CANTENAC
LA LAGUNE	LUDON
DESMIRAIL	MARGAUX
CALON-SÉGUR	ST. ESTÈPHE
FERRIÈRE	MARGAUX
MARQUIS-D'ALESME-BECKER	MARGAUX
BOYD-CANTENAC	MARGAUX

Fourth Growths

ST. PIERRE (BONTEMPS AND SEVAISTRE)	ST. JULIEN
BRANAIRE-(DULUC)-DUCRU	ST. JULIEN
TALBOT	ST. JULIEN
DUHART-MILON	PAUILLAC
POUJET	CANTENAC
ROCHET	ST. ESTÈPHE
LA TOUR-CARNET	ST. LAURENT
BEYCHEVELLE	ST. JULIEN
LE PRIEURÉ	CANTENAC
MARQUIS DE TERME (OR THERME)	MARGAUX

Fifth Growths

PONTET-CANET	PAUILLAC
BATAILLEY	PAUILLAC
GRAND-PUY-LACOSTE	PAUILLAC
GRAND-PUY-DUCASSE	PAUILLAC
LYNCH-BAGES	PAUILLAC
LYNCH-MOUSSAS	PAUILLAC
DAUZAC	LABARDE
MOUTON D'ARMAILHACQ	PAUILLAC
LE TERTRE	ARSAC
HAUT-BAGES-LIBÉRAL	PAUILLAC
PÉDESCLAUX	PAUILLAC
BELGRAVE	ST. LAURENT
CAMENSAC	ST. LAURENT
COS LABORY	ST. ESTÈPHE
CLERC-MILON	PAUILLAC
CROIZET-BAGES	PAUILLAC
CANTEMERLE	MACAU

2. SAINT ÉMILION

Saint Émilion Premier Grand Cru Classé

CHÂTEAU AUSONE   CHÂTEAU CHEVAL-BLANC

Château   *Château*
BEAUSÉJOUR (DUFAU)   BEAUSEJOUR (FAGOUET)
BELAIR   CANON
CLOS FOURTET   FIGEAC
LA GAFFELIÈRE-NAUDES   MAGDELAINE
PAVIE   TROTTEVIEILLE

Saint Émilion Grand Cru Classé

Château   *Château*
L'ANGELUS   BALESTARD LA TONNELLE
BELLEVUE   CADET BON
CADET PIÔLA   CANON LA GAFFELIÈRE
CAP DE MOURLIN   CHAPELLE MADELEINE
CHAUVIN   CORBIN (GIRAUD)
CORBIN MICHOTTE   COUTET
CROQUE MICHOTTE   CURÉ BON
FANPLEGADE   FONROQUE
FRANC MAYNE   GRAND BARRAIL LAMARZELLE
GRAND CORBIN DESPAGNE   FIGEAC
GRAND CORBIN PECRESSE   GRAND MAYNE
GRAND PORTET   GRAND MURAILLES
GUADET SAINT JULIEN   JEAN FAURE
GLOS DES JACOBINS   LA CARTE
LA CLOTTE   LA CLUSIÈRE
LA COUSPAUDE   LA DOMINIQUE
LARCIS DUCASSE   LARMARZELLE
LARMANDE   LAROZE
LASSERRE   LA TOUR DU PIN FIGEAC
LA TOUR DU PIN FIGEAC (MOUEIX)   (BÉLIVIER)
LA TOUR FIGEAC   LE CHATELET
LE COUVENT   LE PRIEURÉ
MAUVEZIN   MOULIN DU CADET
PAVIE DECESSE   PAVIE MACQUIN
PAVILLON CADET   PETIT FAURIE DE BOUCHARD
PETIT FAURIE DE SOUTARD   RIPEAU
SANSONNET   SAINT GEORGES CÔTE PAVIE
CLOS SAINT MARTIN   TERTRE DAUGAY

Château

SOUTARD
TRIMOULET
TROPLONG MONDOT

Château

TROIS MOULINS
VILLEMAURINE
YON FIGEAC

Secondary Saint-Émilion Areas

LUSSAC-ST.-ÉMILION
MONTAGNE-ST.-ÉMILION
PARSAC-ST.-ÉMILION

PUISSEGUIN-ST.-ÉMILION
ST.-GEORGES-ST.-ÉMILION
SABLES-ST.-ÉMILION

3. POMEROL

The wines of Pomerol are noted for their magnificent bouquet, dark fullness, and rather greater sweetness than Médoc wines. Among them are :

CH. PETRUS
VIEUX CH. CERTAN
CH. L'EVANGILE
CH. LA CONSEILLANTE
CH. LAFLEUR
CH. CERTAN
CH. PETIT VILLAGE
CH. TROTANOY
CH. LATOUR-POMEROL
CH. GAZIN
CLOS L'EGLISE
CLOS L'EGLISE-CLINET
CH. LA-GRAVE-TRIGANT-DE-BOISSET
DOM. DE L'EGLISE
CH. LE GAY
CH. ROUGET
CH. LA FLEUR-PETRUS
CH. BEAUREGARD
CH. GUILLOT
CH. NENIN
CH. LAGRANGE
CH. CERTAN-MARZELLE
CH. LA POINTE
CH. LA CROIX-DE-GAY
CH. CLINET
CH. LA CROIX

CH. GOMBAUDE-GUILLOT AND
   GRANDES VIGNES
CH. VRAYE-CROIX-DE-GAY
CH. FEYTIT-CLINET
CLOS DU CLOCHER
CH. LA COMMANDERIE
CRU DE LA NOUVELLE EGLISE
CH. PLINCE
CH. TAILLEFER
CLOS BEAUREGARD
CH. LA CROIX-SAINT-GEORGES
CH. LA CABANNE
CH. BOURGNEUF
CH. LE CAILLOU
CH. L'ENCLOS
CLOS RENÉ
CH. PIGNON-DE-GAY
CLOS DU ROY
CH. DE SALES
CH. MOULINET
CH. L'ENCLOS DU PRESBYTÈRE
CH. GRATE-CAP
CLOS DES TEMPLIERS
CLOS DE LA GRAVETTE
CH. HAUT MAILLET

4. GRAVES

Graves Cru Classé Rouge:

Château	Commune
BOUSCAUT	CADAUJAC
HAUT-BAILLY	LÉOGNAN
CARBONNIEUX	LÉOGNAN
CHEVALIER	LÉOGNAN
MALARTIC-LAGRAVIÈRE	LÉOGNAN
OLIVIER	LÉOGNAN
LATOUR	MARTILLAC
SMITH-HAUT-LAFITTE	MARTILLAC
HAUT-BRION	PESSAC
LA MISSION HAUT-BRION	PESSAC
LATOUR-HAUT-BRION	PESSAC
PAPE CLÉMENT	PESSAC

The most famous of all, Château Haut-Brion, Pessac, was already classified as a First Growth in the 1855 Médoc classification.

There are some fifty other well-known Châteaux producing both Red and White Graves.

WHITE WINES

1. SAUTERNES

The following is the Official Classification of 1855.

Grand First Growth

Château	Commune
D'YQUEM	SAUTERNES

First Growths

LA TOUR BLANCHE	BOMMES
PEYRAGUEY	BOMMES
VIGNEAU	BOMMES
DE SUDUIRAUT	PREIGNAC
COUTET	BARSAC
CLIMENS	BARSAC
BAYLE (GUIRAUD)	SAUTERNES
RIEUSSEC	FARGUES
RABAUD	BOMMES

Second Growths

DE MYRAT	BARSAC
DOISY	BARSAC
PEIXOTTO	BOMMES

Château	Commune
D'ARCHE	SAUTERNES
FILHOT	SAUTERNES
BROUSTET	BARSAC
NAIRAC	BARSAC
CAILLOU	BARSAC
SUAU	BARSAC
DE MALLE	PREIGNAC
ROMER	FARGUES
LAMOTHE	SAUTERNES

2. BARSAC

Classification of 1855: Barsac

First Growths

Château

COUTET

CLIMENS

Second Growths

DE MYRAT

BROUSTET

CAILLOU

SUAU

NAIRAC

Château Doisy, which appeared on the 1855 list, is now sold under the three different château labels of :

DOISY-DAENE

DOISY-VEDRINES

DOISY-DUBROCA

Since 1855, several Barsac châteaux have risen into prominence on account of the high quality of their wines. They include :

CANTEGRIL

PIADA

ROLLAND

3. GRAVES

Graves Cru Classé

Château	Commune
BOUSCAUT	CADAUJAC
CARBONNIEUX	LÉOGNAN

Château	*Commune*
CHEVALIER	LÉOGNAN
OLIVIER	LÉOGNAN
LAVILLE-HAUT-BRION	PESSAC
COUHINS	VILLENAVE D'ORNON

Other wines include:

HAUT-BRION BLANC	PESSAC
DU TUQUET	BEAUTIRAN
FERRANDE	CASTRES
BARET	VILLENAVE D'ORNON
CLOS CANTEBAU	VILLENAVE D'ORNON
DOMAINE DE GRAND-MAISON	LÉOGNAN
BROWN	LÉOGNAN
FIEUZAL	LÉOGNAN
HAUT-GARDÈRE	LÉOGNAN
LA LOUVIÈRE	LÉOGNAN
LE PAPE	LÉOGNAN
LA FERRADE	VILLENAVE D'ORNON
LUSSEAU	AYGUEMORTE
PONTAC-MONPLAISIR	VILLENAVE D'ORNON
TERREFORT DE FORTISSAN	VILLENAVE D'ORNON

Chapter Five

The Wines of Burgundy

by Leslie Seyd

I

EVERYONE who appreciates wine can quickly find a burgundy, either red or white, exactly to their taste. The great variety of character of the wines of Burgundy is one of their charms. With variety goes difference of price. There is a burgundy to suit every pocket.

It is impossible to give a general description of the qualities of red burgundy. There are too many different types, ranging from the light wines of the district of *Beaujolais* to the robust wines of the *Côte de Beaune*. Furthermore, wines of one vineyard but of different vintages may be very different in character because of the climatic variations of their vintage years.

There is, certainly, a tendency for the uninitiated to expect all burgundies to be heavier and more fully bodied than clarets. This is not necessarily the case. Some of the finest red wines from the *Côte de Nuits* may be lighter in all respects than a top growth of the Médoc or St.-Émilion.

In general, burgundies appear more luscious than clarets, because they have more sugar and less tannin. But this difference is more noticeable in the more common wines of the two districts than in the finer growths. Cheap clarets often get a reputation for acidity and dryness.

It might be thought, then, that a wine drinker used to both claret and burgundy would never confuse the one with the other. Not so. In general, and with cheap wines in particular, it is not hard to distinguish them, but it is far from easy with certain comparisons. Be cautious, therefore, in expressing a definite opinion.

In nearly every case white burgundies are dry and have a very clean smell and taste. In certain years the famous vineyard of *Montrachet* (Mont-raché not Mon-trachè!) produces a luscious white burgundy of great charm. In relation to other white burgundies and Chablis in general, this wine is considered sweet, but it is altogether different and less pronounced than a Sauternes or a Barsac. Wines could be produced which might be confused with a white burgundy, but it is not hard to tell a white burgundy from a white Bordeaux.

II

In five distinct and separate areas lying between Paris and Lyon are found the wine-growing districts in which burgundy wines are made. From north to south they are: Chablis; the Côte d'Or; the Côte Chalonnaise; the Côte Mâconnais; and Beaujolais.

The name *Burgundy* comes from the French *Bourgogne*, one of the largest of the former French provinces. It has now been split up into several *départements*, but the name is still given both to the wine-producing areas, which are all included in the province, and to the wines which come from them.

The popularity of Burgundy wines goes far back into history. In the fourteenth and fifteenth centuries the Dukes of Burgundy were renowned for the lavish entertainment of their courts, in which the fine wines of Burgundy played a considerable part. In this manner the reputation of the wines was not only much enhanced in the locality, but was also spread abroad by the returning guests to Belgium, the Low Countries and Switzerland.

Later, with the introduction of the motor-car and the railway, Burgundy became a tourist centre, for, as a glance at the map will show, it is situated at the cross-roads for traffic to all the compass points. Travellers who found it convenient to stay in *Beaune* or *Dijon* undoubtedly took an interest in the excellent wines they found there, and, like the Ducal guests, spread the news of them abroad. With such political and geographical aids, and with the active salesmanship of the Burgundian merchants and their agents,

Produce of Burgundy

Harvest scenes

burgundy wines have become universally appreciated by wine drinkers, and their inclusion in all wine lists is taken for granted.

The name *Burgundy*, as it applies to the wines of this district, is not protected by law, as in the case of *Port*, *Champagne* and *Cognac*. On account of this, other wine-producing countries which make red or white table wines in large quantities have, in many cases, imitated the French nomenclature instead of giving their wines names applicable to the country of origin. Thus, red table wines from Australia, South Africa, California and Spain are often sold as "Burgundy," but in general these wines are mass-produced, and while they represent good value for money, they do not compare with the product of the highly cultivated French wines.

As in all other wine-growing districts of France, great care is taken to ensure the authenticity of burgundy wines. Even before the 1914 war efforts were made in this direction, but it was not until 1935 that the *Comité des Appellations d'Origine* was formed. This comprised proprietors, *négociants* and Government officials who, between them, laid down the exact areas and boundaries of all communes and vineyards in the whole Burgundy district. They also set out standards for each wine from these communes and vineyards, which ensure that the wine made in them is, in every respect, up to these standards. In cases where the wine falls short, it is de-graded, and is not allowed to be called by its place-name or vineyard of origin.

Thus, *on the French side*, there is a guarantee with each wine, but this is not necessarily the case in other countries. For instance, an unscrupulous merchant may buy a hogshead of cheap burgundy and bottle it, and put whatever labels he likes on these bottles. It is wise, therefore, to purchase burgundy only from reliable merchants who bottle the wines they ship under their own label, or sell wines bearing the name of a reliable *négociant*, that is, a wholesale wine merchant. In this latter case the wine will either have been shipped by the *négociant* to a merchant he can trust, and to whom he is willing to supply his labels, or the wine may have been bottled by the *négociant* in his cellars in Burgundy.

Domaine wines are those which are bottled by a *négociant* from wines made on his own properties. These wines are the nearest approach that burgundies can get to the "château-bottled" wines of Bordeaux, but, even so, there are very few cases of a *négociant* owning a complete vineyard. And so several *négociants* may bottle wines of a well-known vineyard under their *domaine* labels, and these wines may not be absolutely identical in character.

It will be realised from the above that it is far harder to obtain a genuine fine burgundy than a vintage claret. For every real bottle of burgundy there will be many fakes. But the real thing is worth hunting for, and the easiest way to find it is to go to a good merchant.

III
The Making of Burgundy

In the making of red burgundy two types of vine are used. They are different in character. The first, the *Pinot*, is a delicate plant difficult to cultivate and susceptible to disease; the second, the *Gamay*, is a hardy vine, extremely prolific and needing no special attention or cultivation.

The vineyards with "place-names" (see list at end of chapter) are situated in the best positions on the hill-sides, and are all planted with Pinots. They produce fine wines of great character and delicacy. The soil on the slopes is gravelly, mixed with clay, and contains a high proportion of iron. It is not a particularly easy soil in which to grow the delicate Pinot plant. The remaining vineyards, which are mainly situated in the plains, but to a small degree on the upper slopes, are planted with Gamay plants, and it is from these that the *area wines* come; that is, wines which are not allowed to bear the name of a vineyard or commune.

A blend is sometimes made from the must of both Pinot and Gamay grapes, the result being known as *Passe tous grains*. The proportion settled by French law is one-third Pinot to two-thirds

Gamay. Under present-day conditions, when wines made from Pinot grapes command very much higher prices than those made from Gamay, it is unusual to find these blends.

White burgundies are made from the *white Pinot* and from the *Chardonnay* vines, both of which produce wines of the highest quality. In the lower category, the Aligoté is the vine used.

In 1965 the total area of the Côte d'Or under vine cultivation was 23,000 acres, 12,000 of which were planted with Pinot vines and produced "place-name" wines; 11,000 acres produced area wines. A century ago the total area was much larger, but the *Phylloxera* epidemic and the effects of the last war played havoc with the vines.

Year	Port	Claret	Burgundy	Rhone	Rhine & Moselle	Sauternes	White Burgundy	Champagne
1945	7	6	7	6	6	7	6	6
1946	5	3	4	4	4	3	5	3
1947	7	7	7	7	6	7	7	7
1948	7	6	5	4	5	4	5	4
1949	4	7	6	6	7	5	6	6
1950	6	6	4	6	5	4	6	3
1951	3	3	3	4	2	3	3	2
1952	4	6	7	7	6	6	6	7
1953	5	7	6	6	7	7	7	7
1954	5	4	4	5	3	3	4	3
1955	7	6	6	7	5	6	6	7
1956	2	3	2	5	3	4	3	4
1957	5	5	5	4	5	3	5	2
1958	5	5	4	6	5	5	4	5
1959	3	7	6	6	7	7	7	6
1960	7	4	5	5	5	4	3	4
1961	4	7	6	5	5	5	7	7
1962	5	6	5	6	6	6	5	6
1963	6	4	4	5	4	2	5	4
1964	4	6	6	7	6	3	6	7
1965	6	4	4	5	3	3	4	5
1966	5	6	6	6	6	5	5	6

0 = no good   7 = the best

The date of the vintage, as in other wine districts, is decided by the weather that immediately precedes it. It varies from mid-September to mid-October. Different procedures are used according to whether red or white wine is to be made. In the case of red wine, after the grapes have been gathered and taken to the press, the stalks are removed and the grapes are put into vats to ferment. During this time the pigment of the skin gives colour to the must.

The fermentation varies according to temperature at the time, and will take from four days in a hot year to seven or eight in a cold one. The must is generally pressed twice, and the products of the two pressings blended together. A third pressing is then usually carried out, but the must from this is not used in the blend, as it contains too much tannin, extracted from the pips and skins, and would impart a hardness and rough taste to the wine.

In the making of white wine, which is made from either red or from white grapes, the grapes are put into a press as soon as they arrive at the press-house, without the stalks being removed. The juice is then drained into casks, where fermentation takes place.

IV
Complexities of the Côte d'Or

Drive from Dijon south to Chalons, and the signposts will tell you that you are in the heart of Burgundy, for names such as *Gevrey-Chambertin*, *Clos de Vougeot*, *Vosne-Romanée*, *Nuits-Saint-Georges*, *Beaune* and *Pommard* will direct you to these towns and villages which have made burgundy famous. You are, of course, in the *Côte d'Or*.

The Côte d'Or is the name given to one of the *départements* into which the province of Bourgogne is split. It derives its name from the range of hills, made golden in the autumn, which forms its backbone, and which runs N.N.E.–S.S.W. with a length of thirty-six miles and a height of two or three hundred feet. At the northern end is the town of Dijon, with the ancient palace of the Dukes of Burgundy; at the so uthe rnend, the small town of Chagny.

The Côte d'Or is divided into dozens of communes, each taking its name from the small town or village that dominates it. Thus, there are communes of Pommard, Volnay, Beaune, etc. These are *not* the names of vineyards, but are quite large areas embracing several vineyards. There are sixty vineyards in the commune of Beaune.

In many instances, the communes have attached to their names the name of the *best-known vineyard* in the commune. The commune of Gevrey, for example, has taken on the suffix name of *Chambertin*, the famous vineyard within its boundaries, and is now called *Gevrey-Chambertin*. A wine labelled *Gevrey-Chambertin* has no close connection with the famous *Chambertin*. Both wines happen merely to be made from vines grown in the same commune. A Gevrey-Chambertin, except in rare instances, will not only be a poorer wine than Chambertin, but may also be very different in character.

Vosne-Romanée, *Aloxe-Corton*, *Puligny-Montrachet*, *Chambolle-Musigny* are other examples of the kind where the suffix name is

that of the famous wine of the commune. A great burgundy always
goes under its own name, without any commune attachments.

Let us take an example, because at this stage the position
becomes even more confusing. The commune of Vosne-Romanée
is made up of forty-six vineyards, which will differ as regards the
quality of their wines according to the position they hold on the

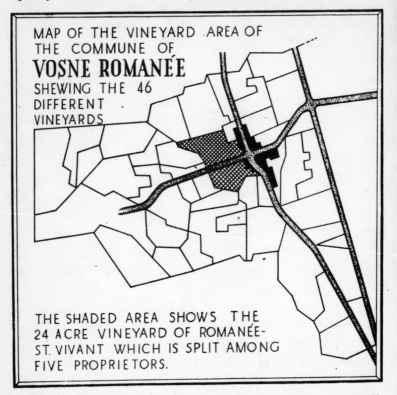

MAP OF THE VINEYARD AREA OF
THE COMMUNE OF
VOSNE ROMANÉE
SHEWING THE 46
DIFFERENT
VINEYARDS

THE SHADED AREA SHOWS THE
24 ACRE VINEYARD OF ROMANÉE-
ST. VIVANT WHICH IS SPLIT AMONG
FIVE PROPRIETORS.

hill-slope. All the wine made can be called "Vosne-Romanée."
Amongst them is the famous vineyard of *Romanée St.-Vivant*. This
has an area of only twenty-four acres, and gives on an average
seventy-two hogsheads a year of fine wine. Château Margaux has
an acreage of 240 acres—ten times as much. Unlike the situation
in Bordeaux, however, where each vineyard is owned by one
person who is responsible for making the wine from that vine-

yard, in Burgundy the vineyards are divided up into a great many small-holdings, some of which are little more than an acre in size. It is easy to see, then, that, since one proprietor may tend and treat his vines and land in a different way from another, there may be variations in the quality of wines of the *same vineyard*, and that wines of the same year from the same vineyard may not be at all identical by the time they reach the public.

Far from modern commercial practice lessening this mix-up of small-holdings within single vineyards, the trend seems to be going the other way. For, although modern tendencies show an increase in mass-produced wines and in proprietary-branded articles which are completely foreign to the individually-produced burgundy, and are, in fact, against the principles of the real producers and *négociants*, estimates show that the number of vineyard owners continue to fluctuate.

Year			No. of Proprietors	Year			No. of Proprietors
1948	.	.	17,963	1954	.	.	17,793
1949	.	.	17,896	1955	.	.	16,882
1950	.	.	19,079	1956	.	.	15,030
1951	.	.	16,521	1957	.	.	11,629
1952	.	.	18,662	1960	.	.	15,100
1953	.	.	17,117	1965	.	.	20,000

With the vineyards split up into so many small-holdings, the marketing of the wine presents certain complications. The proprietors of these small-holdings are, to all intents and purposes, farmers, and the properties they own have, in many cases, passed from father to son over several generations. They do not normally attempt to market the wines they make, as they have no facilities for doing so, either on the home market or abroad. Further, the amount each farmer may make from part of a given vineyard may be so small as to be of little interest to a purchaser.

The farmer, therefore, sells his wine to a *négociant*, and it is this firm who, by buying from various farmers, accumulates a stock of different wines which he can then offer. The names of many *négociants* are well known. They are found, for the most part, in Beaune, and to a lesser extent in Nuits-St.-Georges and Meursault.

V

The Côte d'Or is divided into two parts by a break in the range. The northern half is called the *Côte de Nuits* and the southern the *Côte de Beaune*.

The Côte de Nuits produces about one-third of the fine wines of the Côte d'Or, from vineyards which cover some 4,000 acres. With the exception of small quantities of *Clos de Vougeot Blanc* and *Musigny*, the wines are exclusively red wines from Pinot grapes, and it is generally agreed that individual vineyards produce the finest of all red burgundies.

The following is a list of the finer red burgundies of the Côte de Nuits. A list of others is contained in the appendix to this chapter.

Vineyard	Commune	Acreage
Chambertin . . .	Gevrey-Chambertin . .	32
Clos de Bèze . .	Gevrey-Chambertin . .	37
Clos des Lambrays .	Morey St.-Denis . .	22
Clos de Tart . .	Morey St.-Denis . .	$16\frac{1}{2}$
Clos de Vougeot . .	Vougeot	125
Grands Echezaux . .	Flagey-Echezaux . .	22
La Romanée . .	Vosne-Romanée . .	2
La Tache . . .	Vosne-Romanée . .	$3\frac{1}{2}$
Les Amoureuses . .	Chambolle Musigny . .	13
Les Bonnes Mares . .	Chambolle Musigny . .	34
Les Saints-Georges .	Nuits-St.-Georges . .	18
Musigny . . .	Chambolle Musigny . .	14
Petit Musigny . .	Chambolle Musigny . .	10
Romanée Conti . .	Vosne-Romanée . .	2
Romanée St.-Vivant .	Vosne-Romanée . .	24
Richebourg . . .	Vosne-Romanée . .	12

BURGUNDY

Chambertin
Chambertin-Cloze de Beze
Ruchottes Chambertin
Mazis Chambertin
Chapelle Chambertin
Latricières Chambertin
Mazoyères Chambertin
Griotte Chambertin
Charmes Chambertin

DIJON
CHENOVE
MARSANNAY
GEVREY-CHAMBERTIN
Ouche

Musigny
Bonnes Mares
CHAMBOLLE-MUSIGNY
VOUGEOT
FLAGEY-ECHEZEAUX
VOSNE-ROMANÉE

VINS FINS de la CÔTE de NUITS

CHABLIS

NUITS ST GEORGES
Romanée St Vivant
Romanée conti
Romanée
Richebourg
La Tache

PREMEAUX

ALOX-CORTON
SAVIGNY

Meuxin

BEAUNE

CÔTE de BEAUNE

POMMARD
VOLNAY
MEURSAULT

Dheune

PULIGNY-MONTRACHET
CHASSAGNE MONTRACHET

Montrachet
Chevalier Montrachet
Batard Montrachet

SANTENAY

MERCUREY

CHEILLY
les MARANGES

N

S

THE CÔTE D'OR

It will be seen that the majority of these great vineyards consist of thirty acres or less.

The chief town of the Côte de Nuits is Nuits-St.-Georges, in which many *négociants* have their offices. A few miles to the north is the famous château of *Clos de Vougeot*, standing majestically in the midst of a walled vineyard. The château, which was built in the sixteenth century, has in recent years become the head-quarters of the *Confrèrie des Chevaliers du Tastevin*, which, with the aid of generous gifts and subscriptions, has done much to restore the historic building. The *Chapîtres* held by the *Confrèrie* on different occasions during the year, notably at vintage time, are famous, and have done much to stimulate interest in the wines of Burgundy.

The *Côte de Beaune* produces twice the quantity of wine from its ten communes than is produced in the Côte de Nuits, and the individual red wine vineyards are, in general, larger but less renowned. Thus, the quality of the wines from the sixty vineyards of the commune of Beaune is consistently good, but lacks the delicacy and finesse of some of the wines made in the Côte de Nuits.

The following is a short list of the better red burgundies of the Côte de Beaune:

Vineyard	Commune	Acreage
Caillerets	Volnay	36
Corton	Aloxe-Corton	27
Clos du Roi	Aloxe-Corton	25
Clos de la Mousse	Beaune	$8\frac{1}{2}$
Les Aigrots	Beaune	$56\frac{1}{2}$
Les Avaux	Beaune	33
Les Epenots	Pommard	27
Les Grèves	Beaune	78
Les Renards	Aloxe-Corton	35
Les Rugiens	Pommard	12

In Beaune are found the majority of the well-known burgundy merchants, some of whose cellars and offices form part of the ramparts of the ancient wall which surrounds the town. Of particular interest is the Hostel Dieu, or *Hospices de Beaune*, which was founded as an almshouse in 1443 by Nicholas Rollin, then Grand-Chancellor of Phillippe le Bon, Duke of Burgundy. Originally started with a capital of £1,000, it was subsequently supported by gifts of money and also of vineyards, and in 1647 the Hospices owned ten acres of vines in the best wine-producing districts around Beaune. By the middle of the eighteenth century the Hospices had forty-five acres in their possession, while to-day they own approximately one hundred and thirty acres.

The wine from these properties is sold at an annual auction sale which is always held on the second Sunday in November, and the money derived is devoted to the upkeep of the vineyards and the running of the Hospices. Up to the Revolution of 1848 the auction was held locally, but about that time it became difficult to find buyers who would pay economical prices. M. Joseph Pelasse, who was in charge of the Hospices' finances, was commissioned to travel abroad, and, after two years, returned, having sold the whole stock. From this time on, the success of the auction has been assured, and buyers from all over the world attend the sale. A list of the principal *cuvées* of the Hospices is given in the appendix.

If the quality of the red wines of the Côte de Beaune is, perhaps, not quite the equal of that of the Côte de Nuits, the white wines fully make up for this deficiency. In the commune of Aloxe-Corton some excellent white burgundy is produced under the name *Corton Blanc*. A little white wine is made in the vineyards of Beaune, but this is rarely exported as such. South of Beaune is the commune of *Meursault*, which produces such fine white wines as those from the vineyards of *Les Perrières* and *Les Charmes*, the "*têtes de cuvées*," while the wines from the vineyards of *Les Genévrières* and *Goutte d'Or* have great character and charm.

The village of Meursault is attractively situated at the foot of the hills and is surrounded by vineyards on all sides. With the exception of Beaune, there are more *négociants* in Meursault than in any other commune. Although the commune is more noted for white wines, some first-quality red wine comes from the two vineyards of *Volnay-Santenots* and *Le Santenot du Milieu.*

Montrachet, the most renowned of all white burgundies, is a few miles distant, the vineyards being half in the commune of Chassagne-Montrachet and half in that of Puligny-Montrachet. This wine, in certain years, has a flavour, body and lusciousness that are quite exceptional. At the same time, since the total area of the vineyards is only twenty acres, giving fifty to sixty hogsheads a year, and has eight proprietors, the wine of any one year may vary as from supplier to supplier, for reasons already explained.

The wines of *Chevalier-Montrachet* and *Bâtard-Montrachet*, while not of such high quality as Montrachet, are also well known. The former vineyard is situated immediately above the Montrachet vineyard and parallel to it, and is entirely in the commune of Puligny Montrachet. Bâtard-Montrachet lies on the slopes below Montrachet, and, as in the case of that vineyard, extends into both communes.

VI

A little over a hundred miles from Paris, on the road between Auxerre and Tonnerre, is the village of *Chablis*, in the *département* of Yonne. From almost any direction it is possible to drive into Chablis and find no trace of vineyards, for the area planted with vines is extremely small. The total acreage under cultivation remains under 3000, sufficient to make only between 7,000 and 10,000 hogsheads, according to the vagaries of the year.

The village, which was severely bombed by the Germans in 1940, has a population of 1,870 inhabitants. In spite of the reputation which the wines of Chablis have earned, there has been

surprisingly little development in the area, although some vineyards which, after the war, were put to plough, have been
restored, and acreage under vine cultivation has increased slightly
in recent years.

There are three categories of Chablis. First, *Chablis 1" Cru*,
which can be applied to wines from the seven vineyards of *Les
Clos*, *Vaudésir*, *Grenouilles*, *Bougros*, *Valmur*, *Blanchots*, *Preuses*.

These vineyards are situated on the hills to the north-east of
the village, where the vines obtain the best advantage from the
sun. The whole area must be regarded as very small, each vineyard making only a few hogsheads.

Secondly, there is the category of *Chablis*, this being reserved
for wines made in the eighteen communes in the vicinity of
Chablis itself, and, last, the category of *Petit Chablis*, which are
wines from the same area but which have not the same alcoholic
degree as *Chablis*.

In colour the best Chablis are a golden green rather than yellow
or yellow-brown, and have a distinctive flavour associated with
flint or stones. Like most white wines, Chablis is best drunk
young, when it is fresh and alive, and it is a mistake to suppose
that these or similar wines improve with many years of bottle age.

Chablis produces wines which, being of a dry nature, are specially suitable to accompany oysters and most fish dishes. Owing
to the small amount of genuine Chablis made annually, it is
necessary to pay a high price, which, owing to the demand, may
be more than the wine is worth.

White Chablis is a white burgundy. White burgundy is not
Chablis.

VII

The last three districts to be mentioned are the Côte Chalonnaise, the Mâconnais and the Beaujolais.

The vineyards of the *Côte Chalonnaise* are to be found on a
series of rolling hills facing the River Saône, and are situated in

the *département* of Saône-et-Loire. The area extends from Chagny to Tournus, and comprises about 45,000 acres, the bulk of which are planted with Gamay vines. A little south of Chagny is the village of *Mercurey*, around which are some 17,000 acres planted with Pinots, which produce a wine usually sold under the name of *Mercurey*. Apart from these districts which produce wines with "place-names," the remaining area produces both red and white wines of average quality.

The *Mâconnais* starts at Tournus, where the Côte Chalonnaise comes to an end. The vineyards also face the Saône, but, unlike those of the Côte Chalonnaise, are scattered about, not concentrated on one range of hills. Red and white Mâcon wines are made in great quantities, the red from Gamay, and the white from Pinot, Chardonnay and Aligoté vines.

Six miles south of Mâcon is the vineyard of *Pouilly-Fuissé*, which makes a renowned white wine. The four communes of Fuissé, Solutré, Vergison and Chaintré share the ownership of the 1,125 acres of the vineyard, the total area of which is planted with Pinot Chardonnay vines. Immediately adjacent are the communes of *Pouilly-Vinzelles* and *Pouilly-Loche*, which produce mostly white but also a little red wine.

The Mâcon Fair is another example of the type of propaganda the Burgundians stage to show their wares. It is held annually in Mâcon in May, and is visited by thousands of people interested in wines.

Of the lower-priced burgundies, those of *Beaujolais* are perhaps the most famous and the most appreciated. They are, furthermore, useful wines, inasmuch as they mature quickly and in consequence in a good year can be drunk after having been put into bottle only a few months. The Beaujolais district in the *département* of the Rhône forms the lowest part of Burgundy, and extends southwards almost to the gates of Lyons. It comprises the largest of the five burgundy areas, with numerous vineyards covering the whole area.

The little village of *Beaujeu*, from which it takes its name, is situated in the north-west of the district. The bulk of the wine produced is red and of good average quality. In the north are found the vineyards of *Julienas*, *Chénas* and *Fleurie*, which often sell their wines under their own names. The best-known Beaujolais is that of *Moulin à Vent*, which gets its name from a windmill which is perched on a hill-top in the middle of the vineyard. The vineyard is sandwiched between Chenas in the north and Romaneche-Thorins in the south, and extends over 1,700 acres.

VIII

On Serving Burgundy

Should one decant burgundy? It all depends. If the wine is old and has a lot of deposit, then it must be decanted, or else a lot of wine will be fouled by the sediment and wasted, or it will at least be unpleasant to eye and palate. But if the wine is young and clear, then it is a matter of choice. Some people prefer to pour bright wine from the original bottle, others like to see it glinting in a decanter. In France, the decanter, for serving old burgundies, is rarely used.

It is impossible to lay down rules about the time a wine should be decanted prior to being served. It depends almost entirely on age and on the characteristics of the wine. With a young, vigorous wine the time of decanting is relatively unimportant, but just before drinking is as good as any; with an old wine, one that has had, say, six to ten years in bottle, it is wise to decant three to four hours before drinking, and to leave the wine in the room in which it is to be drunk. With a very old wine, a museum piece, the question of "when" is of prime importance, because very old wines have only a short life once the cork has been pulled. Different wines always need individual decisions, but if decanted an hour before, should be in good condition. Certain very old stagers, however, would be passed and gone if exposed to the air for even that length of time.

Young wines can be left in a decanter for twenty-four hours with little harm, and even for longer periods, but after a few days the wine becomes flabby and loses its life. It is also not very flattering to the wine if it is left over and not drunk at one sitting !

Red burgundy should be served at room temperature. Some people prefer to serve it a fraction cooler. White burgundy should be chilled.

A plain, bowl-shaped glass of fairly large size is best for burgundy. It shows off the wine well and concentrates the aroma. The glass should not be more than half-filled.

The Hospices de Beaune (1443)

Cool wine-cellars

THE WINES OF BURGUNDY
RED BURGUNDY

1. LA CÔTE DE NUITS

Great red burgundies of the Côte de Nuits:

Château	*Commune*
CHAMBERTIN	GEVREY-CHAMBERTIN
CLOS DE BÈZE	GEVREY-CHAMBERTIN
CLOS DE TART	MOREY-ST.-DENIS
LA TACHE	VOSNE-ROMANÉE
RICHEBOURG	VOSNE-ROMANÉE
LA ROMANÉE	VOSNE-ROMANÉE
ROMANÉE CONTI	VOSNE-ROMANÉE
ROMANÉE ST.-VIVANT	VOSNE-ROMANÉE
MUSIGNY	CHAMBOLLE-MUSIGNY

Wines of generally excellent quality:

BONNES MARES	CHAMBOLLE-MUSIGNY
CLOS DE LA ROCHE	MOREY-ST.-DENIS
CLOS ST.-DENIS	MOREY-ST.-DENIS
CLOS DE VOUGEOT	VOUGEOT
GRANDS ECHEZEAUX	FLAGEY-ECHEZEAUX
CHARMES CHAMBERTIN	GEVREY-CHAMBERTIN
CHAPELLE CHAMBERTIN	GEVREY-CHAMBERTIN
GRIOTTE CHAMBERTIN	GEVREY-CHAMBERTIN
LATRICIÈRES CHAMBERTIN	GEVREY-CHAMBERTIN
MAZY-CHAMBERTIN	GEVREY-CHAMBERTIN
MAZOYÈRES CHAMBERTIN	GEVREY-CHAMBERTIN
RUCHOTTES CHAMBERTIN	GEVREY-CHAMBERTIN

Among the other principal vineyards of the Côte de Nuits are:

LA PERRIÈRE	FIXIN
LES VEROILLES	GEVREY-CHAMBERTIN
LE CLOS ST.-JACQUES	GEVREY-CHAMBERTIN
LES LARRETS OU CLOS DES LAMBRAYS	MOREY-ST.-DENIS
LES AMOUREUSES	CHAMBOLLE-MUSIGNY
LES CHARMES	CHAMBOLLE-MUSIGNY
LES ECHEZEAUX	FLAGEY-ECHEZEAUX
LES ST.-GEORGES	NUITS-ST.-GEORGES
LES VAUCRAINS	NUITS-ST.-GEORGES
LES CAILLES	NUITS-ST.-GEORGES

G.G.W.—7

The "Commune" names of the Côte de Nuits:

CHAMBOLLE-MUSIGNY	NUITS-ST.-GEORGES
FIXIN	PREMEAUX
FLAGEY-ECHEZEAUX	VOSNE-ROMANÉE
GEVREY-CHAMBERTIN	VOUGEOT
MOREY-ST.-DENIS	

2. LA CÔTE DE BEAUNE

Great red burgundies of the Côte de Beaune:

Château	Commune
LE CORTON	ALOXE-CORTON
CLOS DU ROI	ALOXE-CORTON

Among the other principal vineyards are:

ILE DES VERGELESSES	PERNAND-VERGELESSES
AUX VERGELESSES	SAVIGNY-LES-BEAUNE
LA DOMINODE	SAVIGNY-LES-BEAUNE
LES JARRONS	SAVIGNY-LES-BEAUNE
LES MARCONNETS	BEAUNE
LES FÈVES	BEAUNE
LES BRESSANDES	BEAUNE
LES GRÈVES	BEAUNE
LES THEURONS	BEAUNE
LES RUGIENS	POMMARD
LES EPENOTS	POMMARD
LES CAILLERETS	VOLNAY
EN CHAMPANS	VOLNAY
EN CHEVRET	VOLNAY
CLOS ST.-JEAN	CHASSAGNE-MONTRACHET
MORGEOT	CHASSAGNE-MONTRACHET
LA BOUDRIOTTE	CHASSAGNE-MONTRACHET
LES GRAVIÈRES	SANTENAY
CLOS DE TAVANNES	SANTENAY
LA COMME	SANTENAY

The "Commune" names of the Côte de Beaune:

ALOXE-CORTON	LADOIX-SERRIGNY
AUXEY-DURESSES	MEURSAULT
BEAUNE	MONTHELIE
CHASSAGNE-MONTRACHET	PERNAND-VERGELESSES
CHOREY-LES-BEAUNE	POMMARD

PULIGNY-MONTRACHET

SAINT-AUBIN

SAINT-ROMAIN

SANTENAY

SAVIGNY

VOLNAY

3. Le Châlonnais (red burgundy)

MERCUREY

GIVRY

CHEILLY-LES-MARANGES

DEZIZE-LES-MARANGES

SAMPIGNY-LES-MARANGES

4. Le Mâconnais (red burgundy)

MÂCON

5. Le Beaujolais (red burgundy)

BROUILLY

CHENAS (LA ROCHELLE; LES CAVES; LES VÉRILLATS)

CHIROUBLES

CÔTE DE BROUILLY

FLEURIE (CHAPELLE DES BOIS; LA ROILETTE; LE VIVIER)

JULIÈNAS (LES CAPITANS; LES MONILLES)

MORGON

MOULIN À VENT

SAINT-AMOUR

White Burgundy

1. Chablis

Chablis Grand Cru:

VAUDÉSIR

PREUSES

LES CLOS

GRENOUILLES

BOUGROS

VALMUR

BLANCHOTS

Chablis, 1er Cru:

MONTÉE DE TONNERRE, CHAPELOT, PIED-D'ALOUP, MONT-DE-MILIEU, VAUCOU-
PIN, VAULORENT, FOURCHAUME, CÔTE DE FONTENAY, VAUPINENT, BEAUROY,
TROESME, CÔTE DE LÉCHET, LES LYS, SÉCHÉ, CHATAIN, VAILLON, BEUGNON,
MÉLINOTS, BUTTEAUX, LES FÔRETS, MONTMAIN, VOSGROS, VOGIRQS

2. La Côte de Nuits

The only outstanding white burgundy of the Côte de Nuits is :

CLOS DE VOUGEOT BLANC

3. La Côte de Beaune

Great white burgundies:

MONTRACHET	PULIGNY-MONTRACHET
	and CHASSAGNE-MONTRACHET
CHEVALIER-MONTRACHET	PULIGNY-MONTRACHET
BÂTARD-MONTRACHET	PULIGNY-CHASSAGNE-MONTRACHET
BIENVENUE-BÂTARD-MONTRACHET	PULIGNY-CHASSAGNE-MONTRACHET
CRIOTS-BÂTARD-MONTRACHET	PULIGNY-CHASSAGNE-MONTRACHET
CORTON	ALOXE-CORTON
CHARLEMAGNE	ALOXE-CORTON
CORTON-CHARLEMAGNE	ALOXE-CORTON

Other white burgundies, mostly of very fine quality:

LES CAILLERETS	PULIGNY-MONTRACHET
LES COMBETTES	PULIGNY-MONTRACHET
LES PERRIÈRES	MEURSAULT
LES CHARMES	MEURSAULT
LA GOUTTE L'OR	MEURSAULT
LES GENEVRIÈRES	MEURSAULT

Principal white burgundy "Communes" of the Côte de Beaune:

ALOXE-CORTON
AUXEY-DURESSES
CHASSAGNE-MONTRACHET
MEURSAULT
PULIGNY-MONTRACHET

4. Le Châlonnais

The best white burgundies of the Chalonnais come from:

BUXY
RULLY
MONTAGNY

5. Le Mâconnais

POUILLY-FUISSÉ
POUILLY-VINZELLES
POUILLY-LOCHÉ

HOSPICES DE BEAUNE

1. *The following is a list of the "Cuvées" of the Hospices de Beaune (red burgundy):*

BLONDEAU	VOLNAY
BOILLOT	AUXEY-DURESSES
BRUNET	BEAUNE
CHARLOTTE DUMAY	CORTON
CLOS DES AVAUX	BEAUNE
CYROT	SAVIGNY-LES-BEAUNE
DAMES DE LA CHARITÉ	POMMARD
DAMES HOSPITALIÈRES	BEAUNE
DOCTEUR PESTE	CORTON
DU BAY PESTE	SAVIGNY-VERGELESSES
ESTIENNE	BEAUNE
FORNERET	SAVIGNY-VERGELESSES
FOUQUERAND	SAVIGNY-VERGELESSES
GAUVAIN	MEURSAULT
GUIGONE DE SALINS	BEAUNE
HENRI GELICOT	MEURSAULT
JACQUES LEBELIN	MONTHELIE
JEHAN DE MASSOL	MEURSAULT SANTENOTS
NICOLAS ROLLIN	BEAUNE
ROUSSEAU-DESLANDES	BEAUNE

2. *The white burgundy "Cuvées" of the Hospices de Beaune:*

ALBERT GRIVAUX	MEURSAULT-CHARMES
BAUDOT	MEURSAULT
DE BAHEZRE DE LANLAY	MEURSAULT-CHARMES
GOUREAU	MEURSAULT
JEHEAN HUMBLOT	MEURSAULT
LOPPIN	MEURSAULT

Chapter Six

Champagne

by Victor Lanson

I

CHAMPAGNE is the name given to sparkling white wine produced from black and white grapes grown on the hillsides around Reims and Epernay, about 100 miles east of Paris. The River Marne, famous on account of its battles, forms the central valley of the Champagne district, the northern part of the former province, from which the name of the wine originated. Real champagne may be obtained only from vines grown in the soil of this district.

The region is strictly delimited by law. Within it there are several very famous sub-districts, each one again strictly defined. The more important are: the *Montagne de Reims*, on the slopes to the south of the River Vesle, which includes the villages of Verzenay and Ambonnay; the *Vallée de la Marne*, with its great centres of Epernay and Ay; and the *Côte des Blancs*, which runs south from the Marne to Vertus, and is so called because its vines produce chiefly white grapes.

Champagne is really a vast inland sea of chalk—part of the same sea, indeed, that breaks out again in the white cliffs of England and the South Downs. Above this great plain rises a low plateau, about 600 feet high, on which the vines grow. The geographical situation of the area gives it a climate similar to that of Paris—mild winter (sometimes not so mild), changeable spring, hot summer and very fine autumn. The average annual temperature is about 10°C.—the minimum temperature required for vine production.

It might, indeed, seem a miracle to find vines growing here at all, far less to find them producing a magnificent wine like champagne. But experience, blended with other factors, has not only overcome the difficulties of the climate, but has used them to produce a unique type of wine—which could not really be produced anywhere else. The vine slopes, for instance, are just high enough above the plains to prevent the plants from being killed by the severe spring frosts that bite into the valleys. They face south-west, thus enabling the vines to capture nearly all the sunshine. The chalk soil, too, acts as a light reflector, and this dazzling white light has much to do with the proper maturation of the grapes and the development of their unique bouquet. But perhaps the rarest thing about the climate of Champagne— to some extent of all northern vine-growing countries—is its effect upon fermentation. Northern grapes have a tendency to retain, after the first fermentation is over, a certain quantity of unfermented grape-sugar. With the coming of spring, this sugar starts to ferment again, after the wine has been bottled.

The vines, too, have been developed over centuries to suit and adapt themselves to the climate and soil. For black grapes, the *Pinot Noir* reigns supreme, and for white, the *Chardonnay*.

These vineyards of Champagne are very ancient. They were there when the Romans came to the Marne. Indeed, the Roman legionaries so developed the Marne vineyards that in A.D. 92 the Emperor Domitian, fearing that the wine of the district would become too serious a rival of the wines of Italy, ordered all the vineyards to be destroyed. They were replanted, however, by order of a later Emperor, two centuries after, and have flourished and increased ever since.

Throughout the Middle Ages the wines of Champagne grew in favour. Reims was the city where the kings of France were crowned, and champagne played its due rôle in the ceremonies. It became, indeed, very much a royal wine, and kings of France and England actually owned vineyards in the area. The wine of this period, however, was really nothing like modern cham-

A view in the champagne country

The vineyards of Champagne

The Abbey of Hautvilliers

"Sur les pointes"

"The Music Lesson"
by
Metsu

pagne. It was a light red wine, without sparkle, tawnier than the
red wines of Burgundy or Bordeaux, but comparable with them
in quality. In time, however, experiments showed the possibility
of lightening its colour, till it became pale, then grey, then
almost white.

It was during this period, between about 1600 and 1660, that
champagne first became "bedevilled." Wine which was bottled
early, and left over the winter, was found to blow out its cork
in the spring, sometimes even to break the bottle: thus it became
known as a "*saute-bouchon*" or "*vin-diable*." Many explanations
were put forward for this phenomenon. Some said it was due to
the phase of the moon when the wine was bottled. Others
claimed that it was the influence of the sap in the vines rising
again in the spring. Others—and their opinion is held in much
respect to-day—claimed that it had something to do with the vine
chalky soil of Champagne.

It was left to one man, not precisely to discover sparkling
champagne or even to explain its causes, but to use the phenomenon of the *saute-bouchon* as a means of producing a very rare
wine. The famous Dom Pérignon, a monk of the Benedictine
Monastery of Hautvilliers, in the heart of Champagne, became
the cellarer of the monastery in 1670, and began a series of
experiments the results of which are accepted to-day, and upon
which the making of sparkling champagne still depends. Dom
Pérignon devised means of clarification of the wine, introduced
a better method of corking, laid down rules about temperature,
and—greatest of all—invented the *cuvée*; that is, the method of
blending different wines from various growths of the Champagne
district into an harmonious drink. From then on, sparkling
champagne increased in popularity—a popularity which endures
to this day.

II

The cultivation of the vine in Champagne is costly and requires
great care. After suitable ground has been prepared and the vine

planted, it takes five or six years before one can obtain grapes of the right quality; the vine remains productive for between twenty and thirty years. In some vintages, owing to spring frosts or insects in the summer, the vines may produce hardly any grapes of the right quality; but even in these years it is necessary to give the vines the same care and attention.

Champagne is a blended wine. There are, consequently, no individual names corresponding to the vineyards of Burgundy or the châteaux of Bordeaux. All the wines are blended by the great Champagne firms, who generally have their own vineyards, and are sold under their names. Before the end of September, or early in October, the grape-gathering takes place. This is the time to pick the grapes, while they are at their best period of ripeness. However, one must be careful not to wait too long, for at the end of the vintage the grapes become over-ripe and impart a dark tint to the wine.

If you visit the vineyards at vintage time, you will see how carefully the grapes are cut off the vines with a hooked knife. Then they pass through the hands of a group of women, specially trained in the work of pulling off the decayed, unripe or otherwise unsound grapes. This process is most important and involves considerable expense.

In the press-house the grapes are pressed in lots of approximately 4,000 kilograms, each lot producing about thirteen 200-litre casks of wine. The amount of must allowed to be extracted from fixed quantities of grapes is controlled by law. The first ten casks are known as *Vin de Cuvée*, and make the finest wine; the last three, called *tailles*, make a slightly poorer wine, called *Vin de Suite*. Later pressings of the grapes produce a must called *rebêche*, but the wine made from this is not allowed to be sold as champagne: it has a reputation of making those who drink it very short of temper!

You will notice that, while champagne is a white wine, it is made from black as well as from white grapes. The black colour

CHAMPAGNE

CHAMPAGNE

1 Montagne de Reims.
2 Vallée de la Marne
3 La Côte des Blancs.
4 Vallée de Marne et Aisne

resides entirely in the skins, and this explains why pressing must be prompt, in order to separate the juice from the skin, and to avoid what is called a "stained wine," that is to say, a wine of a light pinkish shade. Should something happen to go wrong and the wine be stained, it is useless for the *cuvée*.

The must is run off into barrels, which are taken to the cellars of the producers; from this moment onwards, until it appears as champagne on your table, it requires the greatest care. A young wine, like a baby, is a living thing, and will improve; but unless properly "nursed", it will not mature into the fine wine we all expect.

If the summer has been fine with plenty of sun, the grapes, well ripened, will produce a wine of high quality. This you may find on the market as vintage wine, a blend of the best growths in an exceptional year. But some of these exceptionally good wines are kept for blending with wines of other vintages, the quality of which may not have reached the same high standard. Thus the best non-vintage wines are made, which show remarkable consistency from one year to the next, and which are somewhat lighter in body than vintage champagne, but which nevertheless mature extremely well.

It is far easier to remember the name or the label of a non-vintage than particular years which have been selected as vintages, and have become famous.

The best guarantee of reliability in a non-vintage champagne is the shippers' label: these wines often represent better value than the more expensive vintage wines.

Within about three weeks of the arrival of the casks in the cellars, the grape-juice becomes wine, but contains a sediment, due to the fermentation. At this stage, the doors and windows of the cellars are opened, so as to allow the cold air to surround the casks; the consequent fall in temperature facilitates the deposit of the sediment. When this has fallen to the bottom of the cask, comes the racking, which separates the wine from the dregs.

Immediately after racking, all the wines from the same vineyard are poured into enormous vats, which have huge wooden mixers calculated to ensure a homogeneous wine for each vineyard. After this mixing process the wine is again poured into casks, and rests there for a month or two. This period is devoted to a process which demands the whole experience of the firm— the blending of the *cuvée*. In Champagne, wines of different vineyards are blended in certain proportions; the wine of one vineyard will give the strength; another, the refined quality; a third, delicacy; the fourth, a particular bouquet; and the last one will harmonise the whole. But with too much of one and not enough of another, the required character will not be achieved. To blend a perfect *cuvée*, the only instruments at our disposal are the palate and the nose.

In fact, the wine is tasted again and again, until it meets with the entire approval of all the appraisers; after that, this operation, done at first on a small scale, will be carried out on a much larger scale in those enormous vats already mentioned.

III

Some people believe that the bubbles in champagne—the *mousse*—have been artificially obtained. If this is a practice in certain countries, in Champagne it is certainly not the case. In the process of fermentation the wine itself produces, quite naturally, carbonic acid gas, which gives the wine its sparkle and froth. This fermentation, of course, must take place after the wine has been bottled, otherwise the gas would escape—as it does during the normal, or first, fermentation of all wines.

To explain fermentation in bottle, it must be said that the new wines contain, at a dormant stage, ferments which may develop when placed in favourable conditions. Just as a human being needs certain kinds of food, so the wine, in order to ferment in bottle, requires a little extra sugar. The sugar used is pure cane-sugar only; it is dissolved in the very best wine of the oldest *cuvées*; and this is the only thing that is added at the time of bottling, before the bottles are corked and stacked in cellars where the temperature remains constant.

Within a few days the ferments begin to work on the sugar, producing alcohol and natural carbon dioxide; since the bottles are securely corked, the gas cannot escape and is retained in the wine. Fermentation in bottle takes at least three months. The *mousse* resulting from this fermentation must be neither too little nor too great: the real connoisseur appreciates a wine without a great deal of froth.

After the *mousse* has been obtained, the bottle contains wine with its natural bubble. But the wine is "cloudy" and must be made clear, or "bright", before it is sold. To achieve this, one cannot decant champagne in the same way as claret or port, because of the pressure inside the bottle. The bottles have to be placed *"sur pointes"*, that is, with the neck down at an angle of 45 degrees, in special racks or *"pupitres."* Virtually every day they will be shaken or turned, until all the sediment has settled on the cork, by which time the bottle is upside down. This work may be lengthy but does not usually exceed 3 or 4 months. The men who manipulate the bottles are called the *"remueurs"*. In the cellars they are usually known as *"les musiciens"* on account of the peculiar rhythmic tune you can hear whilst the bottles are being turned. Each man handles about 40,000 bottles a day.

When the wine is perfectly clear, another workman, holding the neck of the bottle downwards, removes the iron fastening which holds the cork fast, and brings the bottle deftly into a horizontal position; thus the cork pops out with great force, and is followed by the sediment which is clinging to it. This work requires great dexterity; if the cork is taken out too quickly, a considerable quantity of the wine escapes, and is wasted; whilst, if the bottle is uncorked too slowly, the sediment falls back into the bottle and the wine is cloudy. Machines have been tried, but less successfully, for only a man can do this properly; and he has, further, to try the wine to ascertain if it has any bad flavour, or if it is corky.

Immediately after the sediment has been ejected, another man, with the aid of a special machine, entirely silvered, pours into the bottle the necessary amount of liqueur, made, as previously explained, from sugar and the best old wine. The quantity of liqueur varies according to the type of wine required—rich, "sec", or dry, as the case may be.

The bottles are now recorked with a new cork cut from the best bark, bearing the name of the firm, and the word "Champagne", as required by French law; and the cork is then fastened in position with wire. By this time the bottle is practically ready. The wine itself is not ready, and must be allowed to rest horizontally for six months or more before being suitable for consumption. After this rest period, and according to the orders on hand, the bottles are carefully inspected; those that are not perfect, owing to slight sediment or to faulty corking, are set aside. The bottles that have been passed are labelled and packed for shipment.

The champagne you drink is the result of great care spread over many years. To show good quality and well-matured wine, large stocks have to be kept: this involves large capital investment, and is one more reason why good champagne can never be cheap.

Notes on Serving

CHAMPAGNE

The ideal temperature at which to keep champagne varies between 5°C. and 8°C. The type of glass commonly used in France is as illustrated—but the bowl-shaped glass is perhaps more common in this country. To use flat glasses is a mistake.

Among the best recent vintages—the great 1928 being now a thing of the past—are 1934, '37, '43, '45, '47, and '49, '52, '53, and '55,'59, '61, '62, '64, '66, '69.

If you drink champagne as it should be drunk (that is to say cool, but not over-iced), you will enjoy one of the best things that the soil and the vine, with human aid, can produce—a present from Heaven. Champagne makes everything look easy and everyone feel young and happy.

The principal champagne shippers include the following: Ayala, Bollinger, Charles Heidsieck, Heidsieck Monopole, Krug, Lanson, Mumem, Moët & Chandon, Piper-Heidsieck, Perrier Jouet, Pommery, Pol Roger, Roederer, Veuve Clicquot.

Fine examples of silver wine-labels. They came into vogue in the 18th century
with the introduction of the decanter

Rare Namens

The label "Nig" was used by 19th-century snobs who did not wish their servants to know they were drinking gin!

Hungary

Hungary makes several good wines, the best-known of which are all white.

The supreme wine of Hungary is *Tokay*. The really great Tokay, a wine made with all the care of the finest *Trockenbeeren-auslese*, is called Tokay Essence, or *Tokaij Essencia*. This, indeed, is hardly a wine, and is more suited to the admiration of a liqueur glass. Next comes the *Tokay aszu*, a rich, sweet wine of great power. Finally, and in descending order, come Tokay Szamorodner, a fairly dry wine, and the more commercial brands, called *Forditas* and *Maslas*.

The quality of the wine is determined by the amount of *trockenbeeren* grapes used in its making, noted on the bottle as so many *pottonyos*, varying from one, in the case of a moderate wine, to five in the case of a great, rich Tokay.

Other good white wines of Hungary include *Somloi Furmint*—the *Furmint* is the great Hungarian vine from which Tokay is also made—an *auslese* wine of distinction, and *Szomerodny*.

Chapter Seven

Other French Wines
and Brandies

I

ALTHOUGH, when one talks of French wines in this
country,. one generally means claret, burgundy or champagne, there are other French vineyards whose wines are
quite suitable for export. Some of these wines—like Hermitage—
have been known and appreciated in Britain for centuries; others,
like the wines of Alsace, have only recently attained a standard
that makes them worthy of consideration abroad. The principal
regions are those of the Côtes du Rhône, the Loire, Alsace and
the Jura.

Less subtle than claret, without the nobility of burgundy, the
red wines of the Côtes du Rhône are manly wines—"wines to
chew," Maurice Healy called them. They are full-bodied, rugged,
sunburnt growths, strong without coarseness, with a unique
flavour of gunflint. Their bouquet comes from the *Syrah* vine,
which, some say, gets its name from Syracuse, whence Greek
colonists brought it in the sixth century. A pretty, but unlikely,
tale. Others say it came from Shiraz, in Persia, the reputed first
home of wine, and this is possible. The vineyards of the Côtes du
Rhône, at any rate, have a very long history. Roman proconsuls
first became aware of their quality, while the Papal Court at
Avignon raised them to great honour. The white and rosé
wines of the côtes are, at best, bottled songs, full of sun.
The best are produced from the *Viognier*, *Roussane* and *Marsanne*
vines.

The vineyards of the Côtes du Rhône stretch along the banks of the great river from Vienne in the north to Avignon, with a short break around Montelimar. They include portions of the *départements* of Rhône, Loire, l'Ardêche, Drôme, Gard and Vaucluse. Within this area are found the fine growths of Châteauneuf-du-Pape, Côte Rotie, Hermitage, Crozes-Hermitage, St.-Péray, Tavel, Lirac, Château Grillet, Condrieu and Cornas.

Let us take a short journey, starting in the north. The first district of importance is that of *Côte Rotie*, near Vienne, on the west bank of the Rhône. It is subdivided into the *Côte Brune* and the *Côte Blonde*, and opinion favours the former. The nearby vineyards of Condrieu make a good white wine—fresh, well-perfumed—which goes well with cheese, especially the local *ricotta*. Immediately to the south, *Château Grillet* produces the finest white wine of the Côtes du Rhône. The vineyard is privately owned—many of the vineyards are run by co-operatives—and has only a small production, averaging about twenty hectolitres. The harvesting is done late, in October, and the wine is allowed to ferment slowly for some months. It is bottled two years after harvest, and ages well in bottle. It is a fairly dry, heady wine, not unlike some Rhine wines, but with more body. Thè chestnuts of the Ardêche make an excellent accompaniment.

South again down the river, to where a steep terraced hill thrusts out and bends the stream. The hill of Hermitage. Its slopes are so steep that all work is extremely arduous. The vineyards of *Hermitage*—including those of *Crozes-Hermitage*, *Mercurol* and *Les Chassis*—suffered very greatly from the *Phylloxera*, and it is no good pretending that they have ever fully recovered their former standards. But the wine, both the red and the white, is still good. The red is made exclusively from the Syrah. It is a heady, spirituous wine, magnificently deep ruby in colour, blending towards amethyst, mellow and fine. A well-cooked partridge goes excellently with it. It brings out its strong savour and lingers on the palate. For the white Hermitage, a fresh pike.

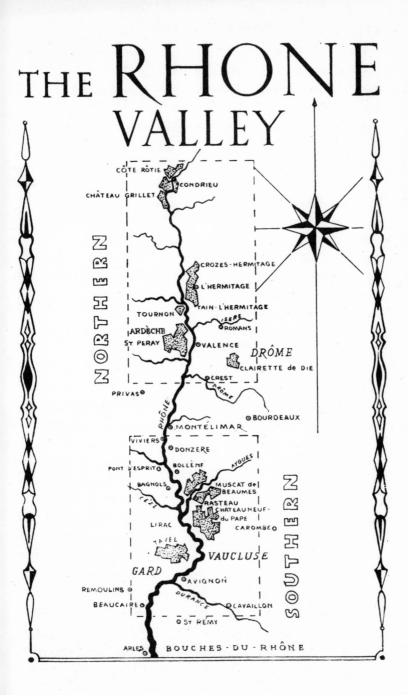

THE RHÔNE VALLEY

CÔTE ROTIE
CONDRIEU
CHÂTEAU GRILLET

NORTHERN

CROZES·HERMITAGE
L'HERMITAGE
TAIN·L'HERMITAGE
ISÈRE
TOURNON
ROMANS
ARDÈCHE
ST PERAY
VALENCE
DRÔME
CLAIRETTE de DIE
CREST
DRÔME
PRIVAS
BOURDEAUX
RHÔNE
MONTÉLIMAR
VIVIERS
DONZÈRE
PONT D'ESPRIT
BOLLÈNE
AYGUES
BAGNOLS
MUSCAT de
BEAUMES
CÈZE
RASTEAU
CHATEAUNEUF·
du PAPE
LIRAC
CAROMBE
TAVEL
VAUCLUSE
GARD
SOUTHERN
REMOULINS
AVIGNON
DURANCE
BEAUCAIRE
CAVAILLON
ST REMY
ARLES
BOUCHES·DU·RHÔNE

Cornas, on the west bank, makes a fair white wine, while *St.-Péray* makes white, both still and sparkling. The grapes are gathered over-ripe, but are allowed to ferment right out, leaving the wine dry.

South again, near Avignon, we reach *Châteauneuf-du-Pape*. The "châteauneuf," built by Jean 22nd, stands in ruins, dominating the hill-top. The vines here grow among great round stones, and perhaps it is from these that the wine acquires its delightful flinty flavour. Châteauneuf goes well with game or with cheese.

The last centres of importance are *Tavel*, *Lirac* and *Clairette de Die*. Tavel makes the best *vin rosé* in France, a stronger and drier wine than that of Lirac. It goes excellently with oysters or fish. Clairette de Die, on the Drôme, makes good light-coloured wines, both still and sparkling.

Côtes du Rhône

Place	Wine	Best Châteaux
Côte Rotie (Brune & Blonde)	Red	Wine of Côte Brune
Hermitage	Red	Les Bessards
		La Chapelle
		La Sizer
Châteauneuf-du-Pape	Red	de la Nerthe
		de Vaudieu
		La Fortie
		Nallys
		St. Patrice
		Clos des Papes
		Domaine de Serres
Crozes-Hermitage	Red	Château Clostabry
Cornas	Red	
Condrieu	White	
Château Grillet	White	Château Grillet

Hermitage	.	.	. White	Chante-Alouette
				Les Murets
				Les Recoulles
St.-Péray	.	.	. White (still and sparkling)	
Tavel	.	.	. Rosé	
Lirac	.	.	. Rosé	
Clairette de Die	.	. Rosé and white	

II

The Loire area is best known for its white wines, both still and sparkling, and for a few red and rosé wines as well. The total area of the vineyards extends from near the mouth of the river, through Anjou and Touraine, till it ends in the many little vineyards of the châteaux of the Loire and Cher. The principal areas are those of Muscadet (around Nantes), of Anjou and Saumur, of the Coteaux du Touraine, and Vouvray.

The Muscadet area makes a pleasant white wine, not much known abroad. The wine is made from the *Melon* vine, grown in a good clay-and-pebble soil. It is bottled early, and ferments a little after bottling, so that it has a slight sparkle. It does not age well and is drunk young.

Anjou produces really fine white wines, and, after champagne, the best sparkling wines of France. The still wines are called *Vins d'Anjou*, the sparkling wines *Vins de Saumur*. The chief areas of the Vins d'Anjou are the Coteaux de la Loire, the Coteau de l'Aubance and the Coteaux de Layon. As with Sauternes, the grapes are gathered late and are heavy in grape-sugar. The wine is bottled six months after harvest, and ought to age several years in bottle. There are also some pleasant rosé wines, which go well with soup. Coteaux de Layon agree with fish.

Vouvray makes both still and sparkling wines, the former fairly strong and fruity. It goes well with oysters. The Coteaux de Touraine are most famous for their red wines, which are either fruity with a fragrance of raspberries, or have a perfume of violets. They are happiest accompanying a meat course such as veal.

There are many little wines made in the *départements* of Cher and Loiret, not usually found abroad, and also the famous *"blanc-fumé"* wine of Pouilly.

The Loire

Place		Wine	Best Châteaux
Muscadet	.	White	
Coteaux de la Loire	.	White	Au Savennières
			La Coulée du Serrant
			La Roche aux Moines
Coteaux du Layon	.	White	Beaulieu
			Bonnezeaux
			Faye
			Quart de Chaume
Vouvray . .	.	White	
Château de Sancerre	.	White	Château de Sancerre
Quincy . .	.	White	
Saumur . .	.	Sparkling	
Pouilly and Reuilly	.	*"Blanc-fumé"*	
Coteaux de Touraine	.	Red	Bourgeuil
			Chinon
			Joué

III

The little area of the Côtes de Jura, from Arbois to Lons le Sannier, produces many goodish white, red and golden wines. The red wines, on the whole, age well, the better of them mellowing down in colour. The white wines are not exceptional, but are sound enough.

Venetian Glass: A beautiful goblet with blue stem, late 15th century

" Fruit Piece "
by
Claesz

Compare the Dutch glass on the left with the fine example (c. 1650) of diamond
engraving on facing page

A Dutsch glass
1650

Another superb Venetian goblet in green glass, with medallion heads in enamel

The unique wine of the district is the yellow wine, the *vin jaune*, of Château Chalon. By an individual process, which includes ageing in wood for six years, the wine acquires its own personality. It is sold in attractive bottles, called *clavelins*. Another uncommon wine is the *vin de paille*, the "straw wine," whose grapes, like those of sherry, are ripened, after gathering, by being exposed on mats to the sun. It is high in both sugar and alcohol.

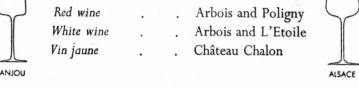

WINES OF THE JURA

Red wine	. .	Arbois and Poligny
White wine	. .	Arbois and L'Etoile
Vin jaune	. .	Château Chalon

ANJOU   ALSACE

IV

The wines of Alsace are gradually making their name abroad. They are all white, and the best of them are very good. The wines are usually classed and named according to the type and quality of the vine from which they are made. As there is no "château-bottling" in Alsace, the wines, which are blended, are sold under the name of the merchant and shipper. The best way, therefore, to get a good Alsace is to get a good merchant.

The chief vines are the Traminer, the Riesling, the Sylvaner and the Pinot. The best wines are the Traminer and the Gewürztraminer, which are mellow, rich and aromatic. A Gewürztraminer of a good year, "Grande Reserve" or "Special Cuvée," is a very good wine. Next comes the Riesling, a full-bodied golden wine, delicate and aromatic. The Muscat and Sylvaner wines—the latter a greeny colour—are good *ordinaires*.

A few wines go out with the name of their district of origin on the label, but this is fairly rare. Ribeauvillé, Riquewihr, Thann and Guebwiller are those most commonly encountered.

French Brandies

Good brandy means Cognac or Armagnac. The finest Cognac is better than the finest Armagnac, but a good Armagnac is very good brandy.

Cognac is produced in one area only, strictly defined by law, and complies with a very severe list of requirements before it is entitled to the name *Cognac*. The area has the town of Cognac as its centre, and includes the *départements* of Charente and Charente Maritime.

The soil, vines and climate of the region are ideally suited for the production of a wine adapted for distillation into brandy. As soon as the wine has been fermented, it is twice distilled. The first distillation produces a spirit containing about 30 per cent. alcohol. The second raises this to 72 per cent. alcohol, or even higher. After the second distillation, the spirit is aged in wood. Its fierceness gradually mellows, and the final result is a liquor of such delicacy that no other spirit approaches it. Cognac is really the only liquor with which to end a dinner that has included some of the greater wines.

Though cognac ages in wood, and goes on improving for many years, it does not age in bottle. When one talks of the age of a cognac, therefore, one means the time it matured in cask. Cognac producers generally accept the "star" system: one star means that the brandy spent three years in cask; two stars, four years; three stars, five years, and so on. Stars are not directly an indication of quality.

The area in which cognac is produced is subdivided into the regions of *Grande Champagne*, *Petite Champagne*, *Les Borderies* and *Les Fins Bois*. The first two, in the order stated, make the finest cognac. A cognac sold as "Fine Champagne" means that it is a blend of Grande and Petite Champagne, and contains at least 50 per cent. of Grande Champagne.

Armagnac, to the south, in the Gers *département*, is the next

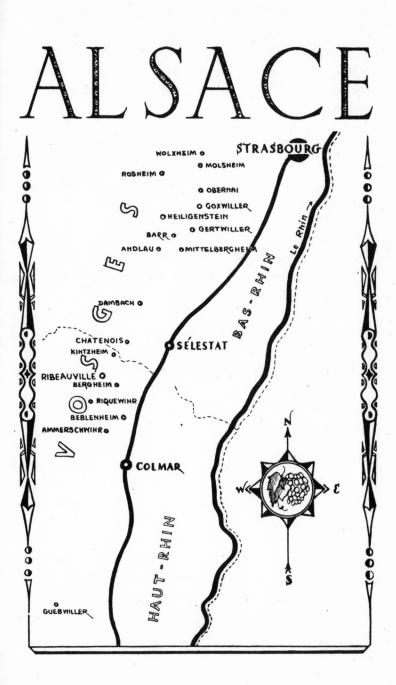

best brandy to cognac. The area is subdivided into the regions of *Bas-Armagnac*, *Tanareze* and *Haut-Armagnac*. The total production of the area is only a third that of Cognac. Bas-Armagnac makes the best brandy, sold as Grand-Armagnac, Fin-Armagnac and Petit-Armagnac.

Switzerland

Swiss wines are not easily found in Britain or America, but one or two of them are worth noting, on the off-chance that they may turn up. Probably the best red wine is *Cortaillod*, from Neuchâtel. The *Cru de la Vigne du Diable* has the reputation of being the finest vineyard. From the Valais, the most important wine-making Canton, comes the *Dole de Sion*, another interesting red wine.

A fine white wine comes from the Vaud Canton, and is called *Dezaley*. The only other white wines of repute come from the Valais. The two best-known are *Johannisberg*, not to be confused with the hock, and *Fendant de Sion*.

SWITZERLAND
Red Wines

CORTAILLOD	NEUCHÂTEL
DOLE DE SION	VALAIS

White Wines

DEZALEY	VAUD
FENDANT DE SION	VALAIS
JOHANNISBERG	VALAIS

Madeira

One of the great and unique wines of the world comes from the Portuguese island of Madeira. It is wrong to say "wine," however, for there are several types of Madeira, including the famous Málvasia or *Malmsey*.

Madeira had great vogue in England until it was gradually replaced in popularity, during the nineteenth century, by sherry. Then, towards the end of the century, the island's vineyards were devastated by the twin evils of *Phylloxera* and *Oidium*. Fortunately, a few of the bigger owners, mainly British, replanted the ruined areas, so that the wine trade still flourishes to-day.

Madeira wines are known by the vines from which they are made. These vines, for the most part, are grown on horizontal trellises a few feet above the ground. The *Sercial* vine gives a dry wine; the *Bual* one more luscious; the *Bastardo* a wine with a fine bouquet; the *Verdelho* a sweet wine, and the *Malvasia* a very sweet, rich, dessert wine.

The unique thing about Madeira is the method of maturation. When the *mosto* has completed its first fermentation, it is put in chambers and artificially heated for a period of three to six months at a temperature of between 90 and 140 degrees. When this operation is finished, the wine is known as *Vinho estufado*. It is then racked and fined in the normal way, and later fortified by the addition of cane brandy, varying from about 5 to 10 per cent., blended to suit the prospective country it is to go to, and then left to mature—for anything up to a century. Madeira has, in common with Tokay, an exceptional length of life, and will go on maturing and improving for an incredible number of years. Since the loss by evaporation is up to 5 per cent. a year, the wine has a high alcoholic content of about 32 per cent.—and is naturally costly.

Malmsey is a perfect after-dinner wine. Sercial, the light, dry Madeira, makes a good apéritif, while the others can be drunk happily at any stage of a meal.

Chapter Eight

Port

by Lance K. Cock

"How goes the time? 'Tis five o'clock; go fetch a Pint of Port."

I

PORTUGAL and Britain have been closely linked for many centuries because both countries have always bred seafaring men. In the days of the Crusaders, ships on their way to Palestine would call at the ports on the Atlantic coast of the Iberian Peninsula for provisions and wine. A force of English soldiery assisted the Portuguese to drive the Moors from Lisbon in 1147, and by the fourteenth century the mutual friendship of the two countries had developed su...iently for treaties of alliance to be made. At this time Po...uguese fishermen were granted rights to work round our coasts, and it is certain that during their voyages they bartered cargoes of wine for the manufactures of this country, particularly w...len goods. Although these early Portuguese wines bore no resemblance to the port of modern times, this trading served to establish not only that Portugal produced wines to the liking of this country, but also that such wines would indeed withstand the journey and the changes of climate and temperature.

From such small beginnings the trade in wines grew steadily. By the middle of the seventeenth century it was large enough to justify the appointment of a British Consul at Oporto. In 1703 the Methuen Treaty between the two countries allowed Portuguese wines to enter Britain at a prefer...ial rate of duty. While finally in 1914 and 1916 the signature of two Anglo-Portuguese Commercial Treaties set the final seal on this growth of some six centuries. By these treaties the British Government undertook that the word "Port" should be fully protected by law, and that no other wine of whatever origin should be sold or offered for sale in this country under that name. In return, the Portuguese undertook to apply with the utmost strictness their laws regarding the area of Portugal in which port may be made and regarding the storing and movement of all such wine until finally shipped overseas. They further undertook to watch over the quality of all wines exported, and to issue a Certificate of Origin relating to such exports, guaranteeing their authenticity, only after their officials had tested and tasted a sample from each cask about to be shipped. It is fair to say that the legal controls in Portugal are applied with absolute impartiality and leave no loophole for the rogue or charlatan. This means that the merchant here can be absolutely certain that a cask or a case of port wine for which a Certificate of Origin has been issued is beyond all shadow of doubt the genuine article.

Before turning to the more practical side of the subject, it should be added that, by virtue of the protection given to the word "Port," the use of such terms as "Australian Port" or "South African Port" is illegal. No merchant or publican may offer for sale by advertisement, price list or in any other way such wine, nor is such a description permitted on any label. The words "Port Type" or "Port Style" are allowed, but the two words must be given equal prominence, in order that there may be no danger of deceiving a purchaser into believing that he is buying something other than intended. No other wines have been granted such strong protection under the law of this land, although it might be better for everybody if they had. The public would benefit in that they would be able to distinguish more clearly between a wine from one country and a similar style of wine from another, while there would be no temptation for the merchant to make use of a famous name on a label relating to a lesser-known or inferior wine. It should not be inferred from this

Wine terraces of the Douro

Harvesters with grape baskets. The leader beats a drum to keep time

Picking grapes in the Douro region

that the wine trade is a dishonest trade. Indeed, it is not. Those who enter it with any idea of getting rich quickly, usually get much poorer more quickly—and good riddance to them!

II

Portugal is a small country, only some 300 miles from north to south, and averaging about 100 miles in width. Vines grow with some success in many areas north of Lisbon, mostly on the coastal plains. Here the soil is alluvial and more suited to the growing of corn than to wine of high distinction. However, it was from grapes grown here—mainly in the extreme north of present-day Portugal—that the wines were made which first came to Britain many hundreds of years ago. These wines were full of colour, rich and fruity, and approximated more to burgundy than to port as we know it. They served a good purpose, but were gradually superseded by wines from a more rugged, wild and mountainous region lying well inland, which was probably first visited by English traders during the latter half of the seventeenth century. This transfer from one area to another marked the start of the growth of the modern port wine trade.

The area referred to is known colloquially as "the Douro." The Douro is, in fact, a river, which rises in Spain, where it is called the Duero, and in due course reaches the Portuguese frontier about thirty miles from its northern extremity and then is itself the frontier for about forty miles. It then flows due west through very mountainous country, eventually reaching the sea about three miles west of Oporto, the second city of Portugal and the centre of the port trade. The area in which port may be made, and which is legally demarcated as has already been mentioned, commences some forty-five miles inland from the sea, extends to the Spanish-Portuguese frontier and varies in width from ten to thirty miles. Owing to the mountainous nature of the country, roads were formerly scarce and very rough; communication and transport were by river and by a single-line railway winding up the Douro valley to the frontier. In recent years, however, great new roads have been constructed. Cars are more and more displacing the horse, which nevertheless still serves for journeys into the the hills away from the river valley. The port wine area is disposed more or less equally on either side of the river, and is remarkable for the fact that it is geologically quite different from the surrounding country.

The soil is schistous, whereas all the surrounding hills are granite. At its western end, the Douro is flanked by a range of mountains rising to over 3,000 feet. This serves to screen the vineyards from excessive rainfall, which in the lower Douro valley averages some 45 inches per annum, whereas beyond the mountains the average drops to about 25 inches. In the summer the heat can be intense, passing beyond 40°C. in the shade, while the winters are often severe with heavy frosts. Thus it will be seen that the climate is an exceptional one, the soil is of a very particular kind, the rainfall (largely occurring between October and April) of reasonable proportions. All these factors combine to facilitate the growth of the grapes which make port. Furthermore, such a combination of conditions is unknown anywhere else in the world.

By no means all the wine made in the Douro becomes port. Large quantities of table wines are also made. These are drunk in Portugal itself and are, in addition, exported, particularly to South America. They are also used for distillation into grape brandy. Furthermore, only a small fraction of the area is planted with vines. In the more open parts of the river valley, the ground near to the river bed is used for ordinary cultivation of crops, while other parts are given over to olive-trees, practically the only tree that grows freely in the Douro. The tops of the hills are too bleak and exposed for vineyards to flourish, and large expanses are just wild, rough country of heather and brushwood, enjoyed by a large population of rabbits and partridge.

The vineyards themselves lie on the hill-sides, which are in

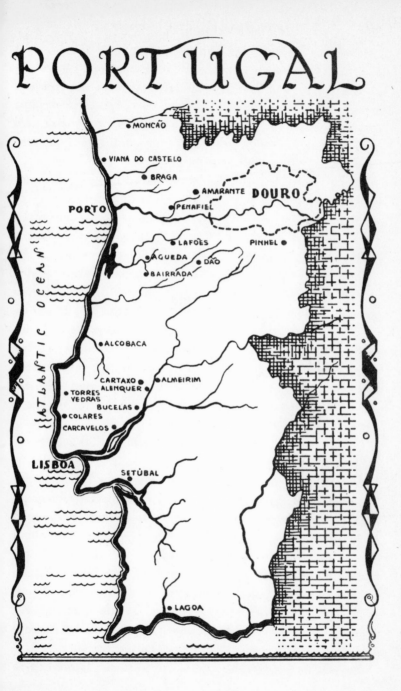

most parts extremely steep. In an endeavour to preserve what little soil there is and to prevent it being washed away by the winter rains, the farmers have terraced the hill-sides. The walls of the terraces are built up of slabs of stone, uncemented, rather like the stone walls of the north of England and the dikes of Scotland. They are often 12 to 15 feet high, while the terraces are seldom more than 100 feet wide. To work in such vineyards is clearly a laborious business, and the use of modern mechanical aids to husbandry is quite out of the question.

The vines grown in the Douro region are many and various. A number of indigenous types of great antiquity, known as Portuguese varieties, are grown; in addition to varieties which have from time to time been brought from other parts of Europe and have been slowly adapted to meet the local conditions. Because of the extremely poor nature of the soil by what may be called ordinary garden standards, it is necessary that each vine should be well rooted and be planted deep. A hole some 3 feet square and 3 feet deep is usually prepared for each vine, and it is often necessary to use blasting materials when planting. The vines are able to throw out great roots, which work through the cracks and fissures in the rock to sufficient depth to enable them to extract moisture from the earth and to remain alive even in the hottest, driest summers.

Originally, all the vines grew on their own roots, but towards the end of last century the scourge of *Phylloxera* reached the Douro. This disease, caused by a kind of aphis, attacked the roots of the Douro vines with the same devastating results as occurred elsewhere in Europe. It first appeared in 1868 and by the middle of the '70s had reduced the annual yield of wine by about 50 per cent. Every conceivable remedy was tried, many thousands of pounds were spent on chemicals and the like, which were poured into the soil, but to no avail. In time it was realised that the only way by which the disease could be fought was to introduce American vines, the roots of which are immune. However, the

American vine was not able to produce a grape satisfactory to the makers of port wine; so it was necessary to graft the old types of vine on to the American stock before the harassed farmers and shippers could feel sure that their livelihood was not to vanish before their eyes.

All this took many years of hard and patient work, but by the end of the '80s it could be safely said that the vineyards were well on the road to full recovery. Nevertheless, it is still argued to-day that the modern grafted vine does not produce quite the same wine as the original stock, although some believe that the American stocks are slowly but surely acquiring more and more the superb wine-making powers of the original. This is perhaps an academic question, of especial interest to the wine trade alone, and it must not be thought, from what has been said, that port is now but a poor shadow of its former self. The difference between the old and the new is in any case very slight, and all that is in doubt is whether, in a really fine year, port can nowadays rise to the superb heights reached before the *Phylloxera* did its fell work.

III

It is not the purpose of this book to give minute and detailed accounts of the cultivation of the vine, but this chapter would be incomplete if a résumé of the painstaking labours of the Douro farmer was omitted. Vines are planted during the winter months, and grafting is done very early in the year, usually not after the end of February. In some instances the newly grafted vines are looked after in "nursery beds," but more often the stock is planted directly in the vineyard and, once the graft has been made, twelve months later, the vine remains in that same position for the whole of its life, which may be fifty years or more. Pruning is done as soon as the vines show signs of growth, and should be completed by the beginning of March. The object of pruning is to allow the vine to develop strongly and evenly, and, most important, to limit the amount of grapes it will produce. Should a farmer permit his vines to be too prolific, the quality of the wine will surely fall. Just as the keen gardener prunes his roses or disbuds his chrysanthemums with an eye to the local flower show, so must the viticulturist control his plants in order that they shall in due course yield wine of that standard and quality on which his reputation rests. Mother Nature reacts with disconcerting speed and directness if the foolish husbandman tries to take liberties with her. Because of the paramount importance of quality, it is also very rare to find that manures, natural or artificial, are used in the Douro valley. The yield of 1,000 vines can vary from 50 to 700 gallons of wine. A vineyard of the first rank should never be permitted to produce more than 250 gallons from each thousand plants.

The climax to each year's work is the vintage. For port this occurs some time between mid-September and mid-October, and the date of its start depends entirely on the weather conditions over the preceding six months. Furthermore, the state of the weather at vintage time is itself of great importance. If it is cold and wet, grapes will rot on the vines and fermentation will not readily start. If too hot, the grapes become over-ripe and shrivel, while the rate of fermentation rises alarmingly or may even be severely checked where the heat becomes excessive. Seldom does all go right. Each farmer depends on his own judgment. Some may start too early; others may delay too long. Indeed, the more one studies the processes of wine-making, the more forcibly is one bound to appreciate that, however hard-working and careful the farmer is during the year, the ultimate success or failure of the vintage lies quite beyond human control.

Not only for the local inhabitants, but also for those who live many miles outside the Douro valley, the vintage is a time of hard work, change of scene and great rejoicing. Families will trek on foot for great distances across the hills and valleys of northern Portugal to work in the vineyards. The Portuguese peasant is a man of simple needs, who lives a rough-and-ready life with few

of the advantages and comforts known to and expected by those
who live in more highly developed parts of Europe. He thinks
nothing of walking many scores of miles with his family in order
to enjoy a few weeks' work helping in the making of the wine,
and joining, at the conclusion of the vintage, in the feasting and
the dancing and the music-making; then to trek wearily home
again to his own small village, already looking forward to doing
the same thing once more in twelve months' time.

The grapes are picked by women and children, and are loaded
into high, narrow baskets. These baskets, which when filled with
grapes can weigh well over 100 lb., are humped on to the
shoulders of workmen, who carry them to the buildings where
the wine is made. Work begins soon after dawn and continues
with only an occasional break as long as daylight lasts. For the
men, who usually work in teams of eight or ten, it is extremely
arduous, as they plod slowly along the rough stone paths from the
vineyards, winding up and down the steep hill-sides. None has
hands to spare for playing a guitar or concertina, nor breath for
singing, but often the leader grips a whistle between his teeth,
and this he blows monotonously to keep his team in step.

On reaching their destination, the men tip their loads into
large, rectangular, stone tanks called *lagares*. These are some
3 feet deep, and are filled to within a few inches of the top. As
more and more loads of fruit arrive, the grapes underneath are
crushed by weight and fermentation begins. When the *lagar* is
full, a party of men steps into the tank and, with arms linked,
moves steadily back and forth until every grape has been trodden
underfoot and the juices expressed. Although picking will have
stopped at sundown, treading may continue far into the night, as
the making of the wine, once begun, must continue uninterrupted
at a steady pace until the process of fermentation has reached the
desired point. Treading will continue intermittently for several
days, and as fermentation proceeds the stalks and skins rise to the
top of the *lagar*. Grape-juice is practically colourless; the colour

is entirely in the skins. When making red port, it is desirable to impart as much colour as possible to the fermenting liquid, or must, and therefore the skins, as they rise to the top, are continually pushed back under the surface, where not only the treading process but the interaction between must and skins extracts as much colour as possible. In the case of white port, which is made from white grapes but is otherwise identical in all respects to the more widely known red wine, it is neither necessary nor desirable for the must to be in contact with the skins. Therefore, either the skins are skimmed off as they rise to the top, or (the better method) the must is run off into vats as soon as the grapes are sufficiently crushed, and fermentation may then proceed away from all further contact with the skins.

In these days when so much stress is laid on hygiene, some folk may look askance at the treading process. In recent years, some Douro farmers have installed machines provided with a pair of rollers, through which the grapes are fed. They then drop, half crushed, into the *lagar*. Men then stand on the edges of the tank and agitate the must with long-handled implements having large flat wooden heads. But the Douro is very conservative and the ancient traditions and customs are slow to die. Indeed, it is not uncommon for a farmer, after using the methods of crushing just described, but finding that things are not going just as he wishes, to order a team into the *lagar* in order to ensure that he will in the end achieve the best results! And, in any event, the wine has a long, long way to go from the *lagar* until it reaches the port glass. Nor has it ever been recorded over the centuries that man has suffered any ill-effects from taking a drink—in moderation, of course.

Now comes the moment in the port vintage which is unique. That is to say, that an account here follows of the addition of Portuguese grape brandy to the must *while it is still actively fermenting*. For no other wine, except those made in other parts of the world after the style of port, is this method adopted. As the

Carting grapes in the Quinta of Meao

New wine on its way down the Douro

A view of the Dou

and its vineyards

A magnificent Nuremberg glass (with cap) (c. 1665)

must ferments, the grape-sugar is slowly converted into alcohol
by the ferments which are found on the outside of the grape's
skin, and carbonic-acid gas is given off. Therefore, it will readily
be understood that, the longer fermentation proceeds the greater
will be the alcoholic strength of the wine and the less its sugar
content. Indeed, if left to itself, the must will ferment until nearly
all the grape-sugar has been changed into alcohol. But at the port
vintage this is not allowed to happen.

The ferments, which are the prime movers in the making of
wine, will not live in any liquid where the alcoholic strength has
been raised above a certain limit, namely, about 16 per cent. If,
then, this limit is passed, all fermentation will cease, even though
the must still contains unfermented grape-sugar. In the making of
port, the farmer, often in collaboration with the shipper to whom
he sells his wine, will test the must at intervals, and, when the
sugar content has fallen to a certain point, the must is run off the
lagar into casks or larger vats, to which has already been added
enough brandy to raise the strength of the resultant mixture
above that at which fermentation ceases. Clearly the sweetness
of the wine made will depend on the stage at which this fortification, as it is called, takes place. The brandy used is of high
strength and very young. By Portuguese law, it must have been
distilled from table wines made either in the Douro valley itself
or in the vineyards near Lisbon, some 200 miles south. No other
spirit may, either at the vintage or at any other time, be added
to port.

It should be explained that fortification is a modern practice;
modern, that is, in the long history of the Douro valley. Early in
this chapter it was stated that the first wines exported to Britain
were somewhat like burgundy. They were, in fact, table wines
in which all the sugar had been allowed to ferment. When the
Douro vineyards were first discovered by British traders, probably during the early eighteenth or late seventeenth century, it
was found that those wines withstood the rigours of the longer

journey better if they were fortified with brandy before departure. But the wines themselves were dry and the fortification itself was slight. With the passage of time, fortification before shipment became general, and the quantity of brandy added was increased. But not until the middle of the nineteenth century did fortification *at the vintage* become accepted as the best method of making port; moreover, a strenuous battle was fought for many years between those who preferred the older method and their more progressive brethren, before it became generally accepted that fortification at the vintage was not only sound in principle, but also resulted in the production of an unique wine, of full, sweet flavour and robust character, eminently suited to refresh and comfort persons who live in the more northerly and more temperate climates of the United Kingdom, Scandinavia and the like.

In Portugal, any property of which the major part consists of land, cultivated or otherwise, is called a *quinta*. Hence every Douro vineyard is known as a *quinta*, and there are many thousands. Most of them are small and are owned by modest farmers, in whose families they have been retained for generations. Some of the big shippers own *quintas* themselves, on which they have sometimes built houses in which to stay at vintage time. The relationship between shipper and farmer is very friendly and close, and once a connection has been established, the farmer will normally sell his wine to the same shipper year after year. This system tends to promote goodwill between the two, and each is the gainer. The farmer receives the help and advice of the shipper, whose wider knowledge and greater resources are a benefit to him, while the shipper can foretell each year the styles and varieties of wine which he will be able to buy.

IV

To return to the wine itself. After being run from the *lagar* into vats or casks, known as "pipes" and containing some 120 gallons, it remains at the *quinta* throughout the winter. During this time it assimilates the brandy added to it, remains at a relatively cold temperature and throws a very heavy deposit in the cask. This is the beginning of the natural process of maturation, a long, slow business for which science has never provided a full explanation and is never likely to. Nor has science ever found any artificial way in which maturation can be hurried or improved. With the vast strides made in our civilisation during the last hundred years, and surrounded as we are by evidence of the benefits of every "modern convenience," it is a comfort to know that the traditions of the centuries and the loving care of many ages of wine growers and shippers are still of far greater consequence to wine than anything else.

The deposits thrown out of the young wine are natural impurities, of which it has no further need. The clear wine is now run off these lees into fresh casks, given a further small dose of brandy and sent to Oporto. The journey is made either by the

River Douro itself or by rail. The river journey, now less and less used by the shippers, is made in picturesque, flat-bottomed boats whose design has not changed for centuries. The prevailing west wind carries them upstream by means of a large, rectangular sail, and the return journey is made simply by drifting with the river current. This is by no means a humdrum, routine affair, as there are many dangerous rapids to negotiate, and in certain spots the river narrows to only a few yards in width.

On arrival at Oporto, the casks go to the shippers' lodges. The word "lodge" derives from the Portuguese *loja*, meaning a store or warehouse on one floor only. The lodges are situated, not in Oporto itself, but on the opposite (south) bank of the River Douro. They are long, low buildings stepped up the hill-side, nearly as steep here as in the vineyard area, but not so high. They have very few windows, and often none at all. This assists in keeping the temperature within reasonable limits all the year round, although water may have to be sprinkled on the floors in the hottest summer weather. The area of these lodges is an *entrepôt*, controlled by the Portuguese Customs, and forms part of the town of Vila Nova de Gaia. All wine coming down from the Douro must enter this *entrepôt*, where its arrival is officially recorded. Once there, it will not leave again until, matured and blended, it is ready to be exported to the markets of the world.

In the shippers' lodges the young wines are tasted and classified. They will be tasted many, many times as they grow older. They will be blended with other wines, which may be younger or older than themselves. And, as time goes on, they will be growing into mellower, rounder, smoother and more palatable wines. All the time, too, they will slowly be removing from themselves their harsher elements in the form of the deposits, to which reference has already been made; and, because the wines are stored in oakwood casks, the staves of which are very slightly porous, they mature in a certain, quite characteristic way, at the same time diminishing slightly in volume. This loss in bulk is only about 2 per cent. per annum, but an important shipper may hold in his lodges a stock of ten thousand or more pipes of port. This means that his stock diminishes with each passing year by some 200 pipes, or roughly 25,000 gallons, equivalent to 150,000 bottles of wine. It is easy to realise from this alone that a port wine of quality and age can in no circumstances be cheap.

v

In a book of this nature, space does not permit the inclusion of a minutely detailed account of the work in a shipper's lodges, nor would it be of general interest to give one. But apart from the skill employed at the vintage, no work is of greater consequence to the well-being of the wine. The shipper must be a highly competent expert, capable of diagnosing sickness in his wine at the earliest moment, and having the ability, through the trained use of his eyes, nose and palate, not only to bring his wines to perfect maturity, but so to blend them together that he is able at any time to supply his customers with wines which follow exactly those previously supplied many months or, maybe, years before.

Young red ports are of a deep purple colour. As they throw their lees, they gradually lose colour; the purple slowly changes to deep red, always described as ruby, then to a lighter ruby and finally to a beautiful reddish-golden colour called tawny. Hence it might be concluded that all tawny ports must be older and better than ruby ports, but this is not so. An imitation of the tawny colour can be achieved by blending together suitable proportions of young red and white ports, so that "tawny" and "age" are not synonymous. A port of great age and quality is bound to be tawny, but not vice versa.

The ports to which the preceding paragraphs refer are known as "wood ports." They are without exception blended wines; their age in consequence is indeterminate, and they are exported by the shipper at the moment when, on receipt by the merchant,

they may be put into bottle. After bottling, they should not be kept for further maturing, but are better drunk as soon as convenient; a time limit cannot be laid down, but after more than six months they tend to lose their freshness. There is, however, one style of port which lives the greater part of its life in bottle, and in consequence develops along entirely different lines.

This is vintage port, rightly described as the *crème de la crème* of the Douro valley, as the following description of its birth and development will make clear. When all has gone well during the year—plenty of rain in winter, but not too much; good conditions at the time of the flowering of the vines; fine and hot summer weather; freedom from disease in the vineyards; great heat as the vintage approaches, with perhaps a few gentle showers near the chosen date; fine, but not too hot weather as the fruit is brought to the *lagares*—in short, when the gods have for once bestowed their blessing on the Douro, very fine wines will be made in many parts of the valley. From these each shipper will select what he considers to be the finest. After tending them and tasting them with especial care for eighteen months, he will blend them together, consider them once again, and then, if all is still well, will "declare a vintage." This special blend of port, then, is made from wines of *one* year only, and is the only class of port to which a specific date—that is, a "vintage"—may be applied.

When a vintage has been declared and found acceptable to the merchant, the wine is normally shipped when it is two years old. Occasionally shipment is made three or four years after it has been made, but that is not the common practice to-day. On arrival in this country, the casks are prepared for bottling at once, and according to tradition, a wine of 1968 (for example) would be in bottle by December 31st, 1970. After bottling, vintage port should be left undisturbed for five years at the very least, and if possible until it is actually to be consumed. As it is bottled when still in its youth, it is not only still a very full ruby colour, but is also capable of throwing out a deposit. In bottle, this is not referred to as lees but as a "crust," which will adhere to the glass. Therefore, when the time comes to drink a vintage port, it is essential that the cork should be drawn with great care, so that the bottle is not jarred at all, and that the wine should be decanted. Decanting is a skilled operation, but it presents no great difficulties to those who are keen to learn and have a steady hand. Any wine merchant of repute will be only too pleased, upon request, to give a short course of instruction in the art.

Since vintage port is matured in this special and distinctive manner, it acquires a flavour and style which are special also. It is not easy, particularly in the English language, to describe adequately all the subtleties and nuances to be found in fine wines, of which vintage port is without question one of the greatest. But if any sceptic should wonder whether all the trouble taken with this wine, both before and after bottling, is really worth the candle, he is strongly advised to sample the matured result. He will not be disappointed.

NOTES ON SERVING PORT

It is impossible to lay down hard-and-fast rules about port, as no two wines are exactly alike, and what is right for one may be wrong for another. The following notes are generalisations, and could probably all be disproved in particular cases.

Summary of Types of Port

Vintage Port: The finest port wine, made with the grapes of one —exceptionally fine—vintage. The wine is shipped to England and bottled in its second year. It matures in bottle, and should not be drunk for at least five—better fifteen—years after bottling. It is the only port to bear a vintage-year label.

Crusted Port: The "next best thing" to a vintage port. It is nearly always a blend of several years, but may on occasion be a blend of wines of one year. It is shipped when quite young, and,

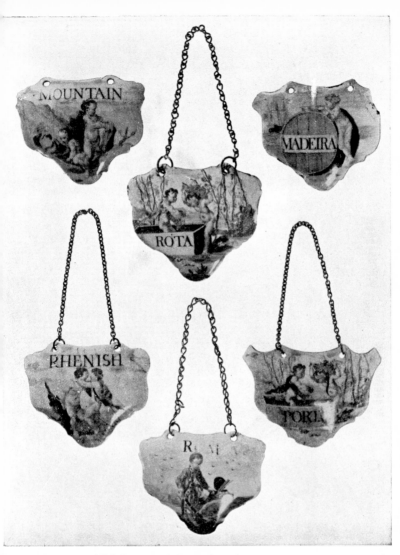

Six Battersea enamel labels, printed from plates by Simon François Ravenet. The Ravenet labels are the finest and rarest examples of the art

More Ravenet labels, from the Ionides Collection

therefore still full of colour and body. It is bottled immediately after shipment, and usually reaches its best at between five and ten years after bottling. It is therefore a wine after the style of a vintage port, but not with the same very high quality and keeping powers. It is cheaper than vintage port for these reasons. A crusted wine will not have the very full luscious flavour and breed of a vintage, but it shows bottle flavour, and is therefore quite different from wood ports, from which it makes an agreeable change.

Wood Ports: Non-vintage blended wines, matured in wood in Portugal. A young wood port is a ruby port. With age, it loses some of its depth of colour, mellows, improves and becomes a tawny port. Much so-called tawny, however, is a mere blend of ruby and white ports.

The Decanting of Port

Vintage Port (and Crusted Port): The bottle, in being taken from the bin, must be kept in the position in which it lay. In drawing the cork, the bottle should not be tilted above about 30 degrees from the horizontal. The wine should be poured out with the greatest care, and the bottle should not be jarred in any way. If, however, little pieces of crust do break loose and enter the decanter, they will not do any harm to the wine. If a silver or muslin filter is used to trap any loose crust, the utmost care must be taken to ensure that they do not smell of metal polish or of soap.

Wood Port: There is no need to decant a wood port, but a wine looks better in a decanter, and decanting will certainly do it no harm.

When to Decant

A wine can usually be drunk immediately after decanting, without any harm. If there is any bottle stink, it will quickly wear off when the wine has been poured into the glass.

With a wood port, the wine can be decanted up to three or

four hours before drinking, if necessary, but perhaps the best time would be about an hour before. As a general rule, there is no need to leave the stopper out, certainly not with a wood port, as it does not require to air.

Broadly speaking, vintage port 20 years old or less can best be opened an hour or two before the meal. A very old bottle, that may perhaps have passed its robust prime and is getting rather frail, should be drunk immediately after being decanted or it is likely to fade quickly and die.

But for wines between, say, 25 and 50 years of age there are two totally opposed schools of thought. The one would treat these wines exactly as for younger vintages, decanting an hour or two before the meal. The other maintains that such wine, so long confined in its glass prison, requires time to stretch and breathe in order to acquire full vigour and flavour. It therefore advocates that decanting should take place twenty-four hours before zero hour, that the decanter should be only loosely stoppered for about eight to ten hours, and then placed, firmly stoppered, in the room where its contents will be consumed, with greater enjoyment, at the appointed time. Each school stoutly maintains that its own method is the better, but it is not on record that either has ever declined the hospitality of the other! One may therefore try either method without fear.

Temperature

Vintage port should be served at not more than room temperature. On no account should it be artificially warmed, and if there is not time to allow the bottle to reach room temperature by the natural method, it is better to serve it at cellar temperature. A hand round the glass will soon warm it sufficiently. The same applies to wood ports, *but* in summer a wood port can be very agreeable if drunk appreciably cooler than room temperature. Light tawny may even be slightly iced without harm, and when served in this way is cool and refreshing.

Glasses

Glasses should be moderately large, slightly tulip shaped, and of plain, thin glass. The "claret" size is the best. They should not be filled to more than three-quarters, so that the wine can be swirled without spilling and develop its bouquet.

Life in Decanter

The life of a vintage wine in decanter has been partly dealt with above. With young wines, some will say that they can detect signs of deterioration after twelve hours possibly, and after twenty-four with certainty. This is perhaps being over-particular. There is no doubt that a wine open for forty-eight hours will still be most agreeable to drink, though it will not last longer without losing its charm. A wood wine may be kept for a week or more, but will generally show signs of losing its freshness and tasting flat after four or five days.

When to Drink Port

The late Mr. Percy Croft once remarked: "Any time you are not drinking Port is a waste of time." This may be slightly exaggerated, but port can be drunk with pleasure at any time of the day. Generally speaking, of course, a heavy wine, vintage or crusted, should be drunk after a meal, but a glass of ruby port, with a biscuit, on a winter's morning can be very comforting, as can a glass of light tawny on a summer's evening before dinner.

The following is a list of firms which were well-known as shippers of vintage port for generations; many still exist

BURMESTER	KOPKE
BUTLER & NEPHEW	MACKENZIE
COCKBURN SMITHES	MARTINEZ GASSIOT
CROFT	MORGAN
A. J. DA SILVA	OFFLEY
DELAFORCE	REBELLO VALENTE
DOW	SANDEMAN

A. A. FERREIRA
FEUERHEERD
FONSECA
GONZALEZ (QUINTA RORIZ)
GOULD CAMPBELL
GRAHAM

SMITH WOODHOUSE
TAYLOR
TUKE HOLDSWORTH
VAN ZELLERS
WARRE

Chapter Nine

Sherry

Ian MacKenzie

" 'Sack? You said, but e'en now it should be sherry!'—'Why, so it is; sherry, sherry, sherry ' "—Bartholomew Fair, 1617.

I

SHERRY is blended and fortified still wine made in or near Jerez de la Frontera, Spain, from the fermented juice of white grapes grown in the surrounding country.

Sherry, as we know it to-day, has been shipped from Spain for many centuries, and wine in general for an even longer period. It is on record that in 1587 Drake brought to England, as a result of his raid on Cadiz, two thousand and nine hundred butts of sherry. Chaucer, in the *Pardoner's Tale*, refers to wine from Spain, and Shakespeare, in *Henry IV*, makes Falstaff refer to "Sack." It is extremely unlikely that these wines were anything like the sherry of to-day, but were probably sweet wines. Falstaff's speech is an anachronism, and Shakespeare puts the words into his mouth only because of his own love of the wine. In 1517, the Duke of Medina Sidonia granted special rights and privileges to English merchants who dealt in wine from Jerez (pronounced "Hereth"), and, at a much later date, from Puerto Santa Maria. It is from this date that the importation of "Sack" into England can really be traced. The word derives from the Spanish *seco* (dry), and was used as a term of contrast to the sweet wines formerly shipped.

The word "sherry" can be found in English writings as early as 1619, in Pasquil's *Palinodia*, where reference is made to "a cup of good old sherry." The general use of the word, however, does not seem to have become common till later, as, in the *Bacchanalian*

Sessions of 1693, we find that there "was a pert sort of wine which the moderns call Sherry," and, in Markham's *The English Hus-wife* (1631), ". . . your best sacks are of Jerez in Spaine." The popularity of sherry in England lasted for over three centuries, but then suffered rather a decline. The circle of fashion has turned again, and to-day sherry is fast regaining its popularity.

The word *Sherry* has no protection in England, as has the word *Port*, which is unfortunate for both the shippers and the public. The character and quality of a wine depend on four factors: the soil on which the vines are grown; the type of vines grown; the climate of the district in which they are grown; and the way in which the wine is made and matured. It follows quite obviously that these four factors can be present in one place only, and therefore a wine made elsewhere can at the best be only an imitation of the original. Sherry was first shipped to this country from Spain; it is therefore reasonable and logical to say that real sherry comes from Spain and Spain alone. The word is derived from the Moorish word *Sherris*, which was the name for Jerez de la Frontera during the Moorish occupation of Spain. Wines purporting to be like sherry should therefore be described as "Sherry Type," or be qualified with the appropriate adjective, such as "Australian," "South African" or what have you. It is considered, indeed, that Empire wines would have an even greater sale and success if they invented their own names for these wines, rather than call them after wines which in the minds of the public are unmistakably linked with a particular country and area.

The reason why the word "sherry" is not protected is due to the fact that the Spanish authorities did not clearly define the sherry production area until 1932. Since then there has not been a really satisfactory Trade Treaty between England and Spain.

The Spanish authorities have laid down quite clearly the actual production zone, the vines to be grown, the officially recognised types of sherry, and the minimum alcoholic strength of wines for shipment. They also insist that any wine leaving Spain as *sherry* must be accompanied by an official Certificate of Origin. This certifies that the wine concerned is the "genuine production of the Jerez (Sherry) Zone and is entitled to the use of the name of origin 'Jerez-Xerez-Sherry.'"

The official sherry production zone is defined as the area "in the province of Cadiz which for a long period of time has been dedicated to the cultivation of vines whose grapes are to be used for the production of wine." The regulation goes on to say that "within this zone the best production area is that bounded by the three towns of Jerez de la Frontera, Puerto de Santa Maria and Sanlucar de Barrameda, and which is composed of *Albariza* soil."

II

There are three distinct types of soil in the sherry-production area, and these, in the order of the quality of the wine they produce, are: *Albariza*, which is a hard chalky soil containing a high proportion of lime; *Barros*, a dark, heavier soil; and *Arenas*, a sandy soil. In general, the harder the vines have to struggle for their existence, the better-quality wines they produce—although the quantity will be on the short side. Quality and quantity rarely go together, and this is always the case with wine. Of the three types of soil mentioned, that which appears to be the least fertile —the *Albariza*—produces the best or *Fino* sherries.

The principal vineyard areas, and the usual type of wine produced on them, are as follows:

Area	District	Type of Wine
Jerez Area . .	Anina	
	Balbaina	*Finos*
	Los Tercios	
	Macharnudo	*Amontillados*
	Carrascal	*Olorosos*
Sanlucar Area	Miraflores	*Manzanillas*
	Torrebreba	
Chipiona and Rota Areas	Madronales	*Muscatels* and *Sweet Wine*
	Tehigo	*Colour Wine*

The vines recognised by the authorities and laid down in their regulations for the production of sherry are: *Palomino; Pedro Ximenez; Perruno Fino; Albillo; Cano Cazo; Garrido Fino; Mantuo Fino; Mantuo Castellano; Mantuo Pilas; Rey*. The vine most commonly planted in the Albariza vineyards for the production of *Fino* sherry is the *Palomino*, while the vines most commonly found in the Barros and Arenas vineyards are the *Mantuo Castellano* and *Mantuo Pilas*, which both give a very heavy yield. The vine planted for the production of the best sweet wine is the *Pedro Ximenez*.

Like all European wine-producing countries, Spain was ravaged by the dreaded *Phylloxera* towards the end of the nineteenth century, and the vines to-day are all native vines grafted on to American stock which has proved itself immune to the disease.

The vines are planted about six feet apart, and the cultivation and care of them is the same as in all other countries. After the vintage, small hollows are scraped around the vines to collect and retain the rain. The vines are pruned during the second half of November and the first half of December. The vineyards are hoed continually to keep down the weeds and to break up the surface, thereby helping to retain the moisture in the ground. A constant watch is kept for signs of disease or insects, and the vines are sprayed to keep away blight and mildew.

There is generally a good deal of rain from January to March, with the temperature cool. The rains cease about the middle of April and it remains dry until the vintage. From April onwards the temperature rises steadily, but does not really become un-bearably hot except when the "Levante," or easterly winds, blow.

The vintage usually starts the second week in September, and in recent years the local authorities have organised a *Feria* or Fair, in which tableaux and scenes glorifying the vine are staged, together with horse-race meetings and bullfights.

A peasant of Jerez

A superb bunch of Palomino grapes

In the sherry vineyards

Laying out grapes to ripen in the sun

Carrying sherry grapes into the press-house

III

The Albariza vineyards gleam white in the sun, and appear bone dry and quite incapable of providing any nourishment for any vegetation at all, let alone vines. However, at the vintage the vines are borne down with huge bunches of small white grapes. At the harvest, the vines, at least in the Albariza vineyards, are not stripped of the grapes all at once, but are worked over several times, only the really ripe grape bunches being cut each time. This is important, as the riper the grape the higher the sugar content, and thus the higher the alcoholic strength of the resultant wine.

The grapes, when picked, are carried in baskets, either on the heads of the workers or on a very insecure rickety wooden frame-work perched on the back of a horse or mule, to the courtyards of the farm buildings where the grapes are to be pressed. On arrival, the grapes are not emptied straight into the trough where they are to be pressed, but are put on to esparto grass mats in the courtyard, where they are allowed to dry for up to twenty-four hours in the sun, in order to reduce the moisture in the grapes, and thus increase the sugar content, which is so important from the point of view of alcoholic strength. At this time of year, there are, in Spain, very heavy night dews. In order that these dews shall not undo all the good work of the sun, the grapes are care-fully covered up at night with more esparto grass mats.

When the grapes have dried sufficiently, they are taken into the farm buildings and poured into the large wooden or stone troughs, called *lagares*. Each basket of grapes weighs 25 lb., and a *lagar* holds sixty baskets. The average yield is three and a half gallons of wine from 50 lb. of grapes.

The pressing of the grapes is done by human labour. The workers, however, are not barefooted, as in other countries, but wear a special wooden clog with nails set in the sole at a certain angle, which allows the stalks and pips to pass between them

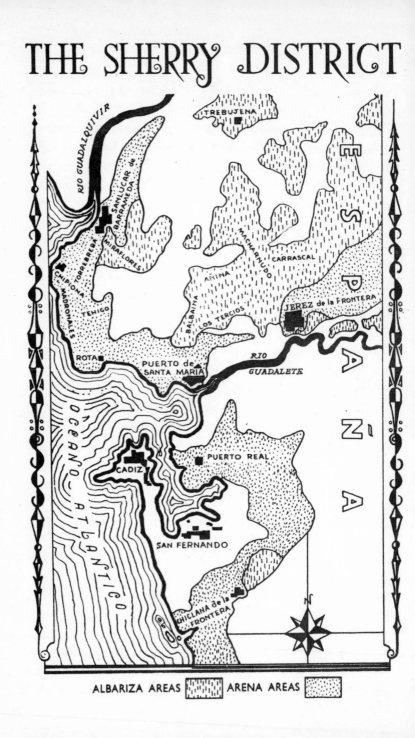

THE SHERRY DISTRICT

ALBARIZA AREAS ░░░░ ARENA AREAS ░░░░

without being crushed. The wine is thus prevented from re-
ceiving too much tannin, which is largely found in the pips and
stalks.

As soon as the grapes are pressed, the juice is run straight off
the *lagar* into new casks. These are at once taken by cart or lorry
to the shippers' premises, called *bodegas*. The reason why new
casks are used is an economic one. Casks which are to be used for
storing or shipping sherry must be properly seasoned, otherwise
the wine will be spoilt. They are seasoned by allowing them to
remain full of a cheap wine for a considerable period. Wine used
for seasoning casks takes on a very woody smell and taste, and is
naturally useless afterwards. By some lucky chance, the freshly
pressed grape-juice which is allowed to ferment in the new casks
does not take up the woody taste, and so the casks are seasoned
without any waste of wine.

The freshly pressed grape-juice is called *mosto*, and almost as
soon as it is run into the casks from the *lagares*, it starts fermenting.
This fermentation is extremely vigorous and lasts from a week to
ten days. Although the casks are filled to only about four-fifths of
their capacity, the fermentation is so fierce that they bubble over,
and much wine would be lost but for the use of tulip-shaped
earthenware "safety-valves," which are inserted in the bung-
holes. It is during this period of fermentation that all the sugar in
the grape-juice is turned into alcohol, and the resulting wine is
completely without sugar and is thus completely and absolutely
"dry." This is one of the several unique things about sherry. The
sweetness of other wines is determined at the time of the vintage,
when the fermentation is arrested at the chosen degree of sweetness by the addition of grape spirit. In the case of sherry, the
degree of sweetness is determined by the shipper when he makes
up his blends for shipment.

The shippers' *bodegas* consist of tall, long buildings, which can
best be likened to the nave of a big church, complete even to the
pillars and arches dividing the aisles. In the place of the usual

benches and chairs, you will find rows and rows of casks, generally arranged in three tiers. There are no underground cellars in Jerez. With the great heat of summer the evaporation of the wine is heavy, and whilst it is essential for the production of good sherry, it tends to increase the cost of production. These rows or series of casks make up the shippers' *soleras*.

It is on the *solera system* that the whole production of sherry is based. The system ensures that a shipper can go on shipping exactly the same style and quality of wine year after year. The real meaning of the word *solera* is "foundation," and a shipper's soleras are his be-all and end-all, the headstone and cornerstone of his business. It would be impossible for anyone to set up as a shipper to-day, as it takes many years to build up a solera system, and at the very high prices ruling to-day it would not be a business proposition to buy up a complete solera system. The old wines in a solera system are literally worth their weight in gold, and are used in very small quantities for blending purposes. Another unique point about sherry is that, provided the wine is sound to begin with and it is looked after properly, it will continue to get better and better with age if it is kept in wood. By the very nature of the solera system, which will be explained later, it is impossible to give a definite age to old sherries, but it is quite safe to say that some of the real old soleras average well over a hundred years old.

We must now return to the fermenting mosto as it arrives at the shippers' lodges. After the first—or *tumultuoso*—fermentation is finished, a steady secondary fermentation takes place that lasts about a month—the actual time depends on many circumstances. During this period the casks of mosto are stacked in the open, or in the shippers' premises, and the casks are left with their bungs open, thus exposing the wine to the air. Wine producers in other countries would throw up their hands in horror at this apparent casualness, for wines treated thus in other countries would almost certainly turn to vinegar. This is not the case with sherry, which thrives on exposure to air, and is indeed the hardiest of all wines.

About three or four months after the vintage—generally after the first spell of cold weather—the mostos fall bright; that is, all the matter in suspension in the wine falls to the bottom of the casks, and the wines are left crystal clear. The mosto is now known as *Vino de Anada*, or "wine of the year," and is racked off the lees into fresh casks. It is only when this stage has been reached that the shipper knows what sort of wine he has obtained from the vintage.

When the shipper, at this point, examines his casks of wine, all from the same vineyard, and indeed from the same pressing of the grapes, he will find he has two distinct types of sherry, namely, *Fino* and *Raya*. The Fino is a very pale, delicate, light wine on both nose and palate. At this early stage the Raya is simply a wine that is not a Fino, and is darker in colour, fuller, and coarser on nose and palate than a Fino.

It seems incredible that from the same vineyard and pressing two distinct types of sherry can be produced, but it is a fact. It is due to a micro-organism or bacteria that grows on the surface of some of the casks of wine, and which, by some msyterious action, makes the wine develop the unmistakable characteristic of a Fino sherry. This mould is called *Flor*, meaning "flower," and when it is growing on the wine, the wine is said to be "flowering." In appearance the Flor is like a white film on the surface of the wine.

IV

Fino, it has been said, is the best sherry. The reason for making this assertion is that the wine itself is by far the most delicate and refined of all the types of sherry, and the shipper can do absolutely nothing to ensure that he will obtain Fino sherry— other than make the wine at an Albariza vineyard which he knows from experience generally produces a good proportion of Fino wine. Fino wine is only produced by the action of the Flor on the mosto. Flor will only grow on natural-strength wines, hence, if a shipper wishes to make certain that a mosto does not turn into a Fino sherry, all he has to do is to prevent the growth of the Flor by fortification, that is by increasing the alcoholic strength of the mosto by the addition of grape-spirit. Thus it will be seen that whilst the shipper can ensure obtaining a Raya wine, there is nothing he can do to obtain a Fino.

At this stage the wines receive their first fortification. The Raya wines are fortified to a greater extent than the Finos, to make certain that the Flor does not appear on them. The colour in a natural sherry is caused by the oxidation of the alcohol in the juice, and as the Raya wines have a higher alcoholic content than the Finos they take on colour much more quickly. The shipper then continues to subject these wines to close examination over a period of three to four years, during which time he finds that he will get further variations and developments in his wines. He will find that the better and fatter Fino wines will have become *Amontillados*, and the inferior reverted back to Raya. He will also find that the better Rayas will have turned into *Olorosos*, and the inferior ones have simply become *Old Rayas*. Some of both basic wines, Fino and Raya, will have fallen by the wayside and become vinegar, and will be thrown out.

The types of sherry mentioned above are the fundamental sherries, and are easily recognisable to the layman once they have been shown to him. There are many different classifications of each type which, however, are discernible only to the expert, and are considered to be outside the scope of this book.

It must be pointed out that these types of sherry are the basic types in Spain itself, and, as already mentioned, completely dry or utterly deprived of sugar, and therefore bear only a slight resemblance to wines of the same description as known in this country.

The Fino wine has already been described. The Amontillado is a fuller, firmer wine—the firmness due to age—with slightly more colour than a Fino, and with a slightly nutty flavour. The Oloroso sherry is a full, darkish-coloured wine with a very definite nutty flavour. An Old Raya is simply a full, coarse, nondescript but perfectly sound wine, and might be described as a blending sherry. The following is a diagram of the basic Sherry Family Tree:

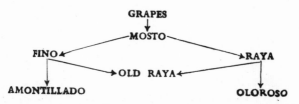

When the shipper is satisfied that these wines have shown their final type, style and quality, he introduces them to his main stock of sherry, namely his soleras. The wines are introduced into the youngest solera of all, and the very young soleras are sometimes called *Criaderas* or "nurseries."

v

The solera system is one by which a shipper can be sure of shipping exactly the same style and quality of wine year after year. This would not be possible simply by making wine at the same vineyard each year for, as has been mentioned, even from the same vineyard, the same year, and the same pressing, completely different wines are produced. The solera system is a means of *averaging out*, and is based upon the fact that an old sherry will always give its style and characteristics to a younger wine of a similar style. It is this fact, and this alone, that is the basis of the solera system.

Each *individual* solera consists of a number of casks all containing wine of the same type, style, age and quality. A solera *system* consists of a number of individual soleras of the same style and type of wine, *but of different ages*. Only wines that have properly developed, and are of a definite style, type and quality, ever find their way into a solera system. Such wines, provided they are looked after properly, improve with age, and so it can be said that the chief factor in the quality of a sherry is age.

The solera system can be compared to the movements of a pupil at a school. Instead of the shipper, take the master, and instead of the mosto take the pupil.

A pupil, on entering school, starts off with a general education. It is only when the master has had time and opportunity to assess his capabilities and attributes that he specialises, or just plods along with a general education. As he attains the correct standard of knowledge he moves up in form and finally leaves. Some indeed fall by the wayside and are expelled.

The early general education can be likened to the mosto stage; the Fino and Amontillado to the classical scholar; the Oloroso to the mathematical scholar; and the Raya to the plodder. These types of wine all move through their various soleras until they reach the top and are shipped, or leave. Some wines will have gone wrong and turned into vinegar—expelled!

In general, the shipper has a solera system for each style and quality of wine he ships. The number of individual soleras or age-groups he has in each system depends on the quality or age of the particular sherry to be shipped. Similarly, the actual number of casks in a *shipping* or *final* solera depends on the amount of wine the shipper anticipates shipping in any one year.

These soleras, or series of casks, are never moved and never emptied, otherwise the whole solera system, or method of averaging-out, would break down. A practical example of how the system works will probably describe it far better than any other way. Let us suppose a shipper receives an order for 10 casks of a wine of which his *shipping* solera consists of 100 casks. The simplest, and indeed the cheapest, thing for him to do, would be to ship 10 casks of his shipping solera. If he did this, he would be left with a smaller quantity of wine in that solera, and no way of making it up. What happens in practice is that the shipper takes one-tenth of a butt from each butt of his shipping solera, blends them together—thereby still further averaging out—and then ships them. This involves 100 movements of wine simply to obtain 10 casks for shipment.

The shipper now has to make up the wine in his shipping solera. He does this by drawing off the required amount of wine from the immediate younger solera—again drawing off the same amount from each butt of the solera. We will assume that the preceding solera is also of 100 butts, and this would then involve another 100 movements of wine. If we assume that there are three soleras all of the same size as the shipping solera—in this example—then it would involve 500 movements of wine in order to ship 10 casks. These figures include the movements required to make up the quantity of wine in the youngest solera of all. This making up of the quantity of wine in a solera by the intro-duction of wine from a younger solera of the same style and quality is called a *"rocio"* or "refreshing."

It can be seen from this example that the solera system, although simple in theory, is most laborious and expensive in practice. It is, however, the only possible way in which the essential "averaging-out" can be obtained, thus ensuring the continuity of style and quality.

In practice it becomes even more elaborate than in the example just given. Generally the younger soleras are larger than the older ones, and therefore each *rocio* involves a larger number of move-ments of a *smaller quantity* of wine from the younger to the older solera than was the case in drawing wine from the shipping solera for the shipment. In addition, there is no question of a quantity of wine being drawn from a cask in a younger solera and being introduced straightforwardly to the corresponding cask of the older soleras. If three measures of wine are required from each cask of the younger solera, then these three measures are distri-buted amongst *three casks* of the older solera. Thus the actual importance attached to the averaging-out process can be seen.

Obviously, too, it would be simpler, and cheaper to work, if the various soleras were arranged one above the other in order of age, but even this is not done, as experience has shown that Finos develop best on the lowest tier, where it is coolest next the ground; Olorosos in the middle tier, and sweet wines and colour wines on the third or top tier nearest the roof.

VI

The wines in the various soleras, as already mentioned, are bone dry, or completely lacking in sugar. They have therefore to be sweetened and coloured to meet the requirements of the individual customer. When the shipper makes a blend for shipment he draws off from an appropriate shipping solera, and then adds the required amount of colour and sweet wine.

The sweet wine (*Dulce*) is made from a very sweet grape which is pressed in the same way as the normal sherry grape, but the fermentation is stopped at a very early stage in order to preserve the sugar in the wine. The fermentation is stopped by the addition of grape-spirit, as in the case of port. The grape from which the best sweet wine is made is the famous *Pedro Ximenes*, and the wine produced is commonly called PX. A wine called *Paxarete* is also used for sweetening and colouring, and this is made by blending colour wine and PX together.

Colour wine (*Vino de Color*) is made by boiling the mosto made with sweet grapes before the fermentation starts, and thereby cooking the sugar in the mosto. As it is cooked, the sugar turns black, and the mosto is boiled down until it is about one-fifth of its original volume. Care must be taken to ensure that during this process the sugar is not burned, otherwise the wine would have a very bitter taste.

Before shipment, the shipper gives his blend its final fortification, to bring the alcoholic strength to that required to enable the wine to stand the change of climate and remain in perfect condition.

The normal alcoholic strength of the various types of sherry is as follows:

Mosto: 11·5°–14·5° Gay Lussac. (Sugar content before fermentation is 11·13° Beaume.)

Fino: Up to 15·5° Gay Lussac.

Raya: 18·5°–19° Gay Lussac.

Shipping Strength: 19–20° Gay Lussac.

(Gay Lussac is percentage of alcohol by volume.)

The sherry is shipped from the port of Cadiz, and the majority of the wine is shipped in cask. The casks used are usually made of oak, and the normal sizes of casks are:

Name			Content	Yield
Butt	.	.	108 gallons	52 dozen bottles
Hogshead	.	.	54 ,,	26 ,, ,,
Quarter-cask	.	.	27 ,,	13 ,, ,,

The shippers themselves do not hold large stocks of wine in this country, and the majority of the wine shipped is to meet the specific requirements of particular wine merchants. On arrival, the wine is "entered" with the Customs and Excise, and when duty has been paid, the cask is removed to the wine merchant's cellars.

The normal practice is to allow the cask to rest for about three weeks on arrival in the cellars, so that the wine can settle down after its journey and come to the temperature of the cellar. Before the wine can be bottled it must be star bright, and to achieve this it is usually "fined." White of egg, isinglass or other suitable fining mixture is added to it, and then the whole is thoroughly roused, and, as the fining mixture falls to the bottom of the cask it takes with it all the matter in suspension in the wine. Sherry kept in cask and properly looked after goes on improving indefinitely, but this cannot be said about sherry in bottle. Young, light, dry sherries should be drunk as soon as possible, and the bottle be regarded simply as a container. The fuller and sweeter sherries do improve in bottle, but their life is limited, as in the case of all wines. It must be remembered that bad wine will never improve whether kept in cask or bottle.

VII

The types of sherry mentioned so far in this chapter have been only the basic fundamental ones as known in Spain. To these must now be added the types generally known in this country.

Before listing these, it should be clearly understood that there is no such thing as a *vintage sherry*, and it is hoped that the description already given of the solera system will have made the reason for this quite clear.

The Spaniards themselves drink, as a rule, only dry sherries of the basic type. For shipment, colour wine and sweet wine are blended with the solera sherries, and therefore types of sherry are found abroad which are unknown in Spain. Examples of these are *Golden*, *Amoroso* and *Brown*. These are Raya wines coloured and sweetened to taste.

The types of sherry shipped to this country, which are very close to the basic types as known and drunk in Spain are:

FINO: A very light, pale, dry wine with a very delicate "nose."

MANZANILLA: A Fino, but with a slightly salty tang due to being matured near the sea at San Lucar de Barrameda. It should be noted that a Fino sherry if moved from Jerez de la Frontera to San Lucar will develop into a Manzanilla, and similarly if a Manzanilla is moved from San Lucar to Jerez it will develop into a Fino.

AMONTILLADO: A medium-sweet, palish wine with a slightly nutty flavour, which, as has been shown, develops with age from a fat Fino wine.

OLOROSO: A full, sweet, darkish and definitely nutty wine.

Sherry Shippers

The following are represented on the Sherry Shippers' Association for many years; the majority still operate

Bertolo, S.A.

Eduardo Delage.

Pedro Domecq & Cia.

Duff Gordon & Co.

Manuel Fernandez.

R. D. Ferraro.

Florido Hnos.

Garvey, S.A.

de Goni Feuerheerd & Co. and
  Bodegas Marques del Merito, S.A.

Gonzalez Byass & Co.

Miguel M. Gomez.

Manuel Guerrero.

Gutierrez Hermanos.

R. C. Ivison.

Mackenzie & Co.

H. de Marques del Real Tesoro.

Martinez Gassiot & Co.

Jose Martinez, S.L.

Miguel Mendoza & Cia.

M. Misa.

Jose Ramirez & Co. Ltd.

M. Antonio de Riva & Cia.

J. M. Rivero

Robertson Bros. & Co.

A. R. Ruiz y Hermanos.

Sandeman Bros. & Co.

A. de Terry.

A. R. Valdespino y Hnos.

Ricardo de Valderrama.

Juan V. Vergara.

Williams & Humbert.

Wisdom & Warter.

The Serving of Sherry

There are so many different types of sherry that one can always be found to suit every occasion. A suitable sherry, indeed, could be found for each separate course of a dinner.

All wine seems better if served in a decanter, and as there is no reason why sherry should not be decanted, it ought to be so served. An old sherry, of course, may well have cast a deposit, and would certainly require to be decanted.

Glasses vary considerably, depending on period. The best general glass, however, should be of thin, plain glass, big enough at the top to get one's nose in to smell the wine, tall enough to contain a fair amount of wine when only half-full. Whatever the shape of glass, it should not be more than half-filled.

Sherry lives fairly well after the bottle has been opened, and will certainly keep perfectly for a week.

Chapter Ten

The Wines of Germany

by Alfred Langenbach

THERE is hardly a country in all the world without some individual beauty in its landscape. This applies to the wine-lands of the world. Vineyards in themselves may not seem likely to stimulate the imagination of a painter, as the vines, shorn of their natural growth and methodically arranged in rows, are enlivened only by the waving of their leaves or by the mingling changes of their colours late in the autumn. In conjunction with their background, however, they can offer quite an imposing panorama, maybe of vast plain or hilly landscape. It is this pattern, unique and renowned, that raises the landscape of the German vineyards above most others.

The picture of the Rhine and Mosel vineyards, as they blend with the rivers and forested hills, cannot fail to impress. The terraces on which the vines are planted add diversity; the vineyards seem to grow out of the sombre woods and often end right on the river banks. Climb one of the hills or one of the quite respectable peaks, and below lies the majestically flowing Rhine, the winding Mosel, the Neckar or the Main, and everywhere in the valleys, sheltered by the hills one has climbed, stretch the vineyards.

These sheltered valleys are of immense importance. It is not always realised that German wine is made in the most northerly of vine-growing regions. Even the Champagne vineyards reach only the same latitude as the southern limit of the German areas. Coblenz is on the same parallel as Plymouth. The sun, consequently, does not spend its beneficial powers with all the abundance of a southern climate. To get as good results as are achieved in southern areas, help must come from other sources, from conditions different from those in the south. This help comes from the fact that practically all the winelands of the German area—Rheingau, Mittelrhein, Nahe, Mosel and Franken —enjoy the protection of hills against the wind, and, even more important, benefit in their valleys from the warmth of the sun which is retained right into the night by the particular type of soil. In addition, the vineyards face south, or at least west, and thus obtain all possible advantage from the sunshine.

We have mentioned the importance of the soil. Its multiformity and variety are astonishing, and every variation produces its own effect on the taste of the wine. Heavy loam and calcareous soil in the Palatinate and Rhenish districts favour the production of big wines, while within these districts areas of light and sandy soil result in more elegant products.

The Rheingau, on the whole, is probably the most individual of German wine districts owing to the country's hard, siliceous earth. The wines of the Mosel, on the other hand, derive their chief characteristics from the slaty soil of the vineyards, in which hardly any other cultivated plant would grow. It is significant that dwarf oaks on the slaty slopes of the Saar were uprooted when their use for tanning had become obsolete, and vines were planted, with excellent results.

The Vines

A fundamental item in successful wine production is, of course, the quality of the vine, which must be chosen to harmonise with the climate, soil and sun. Viticulture came to Europe from the Middle East, but not by transplantation. The wild vine, the *Vitis vinifera* or *Vitis sylvestris*, was to be found all over Europe, in swamps and forests, climbing liana-like along big trees, and bearing edible fruits. It is from this vine that all the present German vines are derived. The *Vitis sylvestris* has only recently disappeared from Germany, and a specimen can still be seen

A view of Deidesheim, in the Palatinate

The Liebfrauenkirche at Worms

Kloster Eberbach, in the Rheingau

A view of Lorch, from the Middle Rhine

The vineyards at Trittenheim (Moselle)

A view of Piesport (Moselle)

Typical views of German vineyards

preserved in the very interesting Wine Museum at Speyer, in the Palatinate.

German viticulture dates from the second or third century, when the Romans, after invading the Mosel valley and the Palatinate, taught and encouraged the art. They knew, for instance, the all-important practice of pruning. Grafting and cross-breeding soon followed, and thus from an early date all the main principles of modern viticulture were employed, and the multifarious variety of vines was developed.

The outstanding wines of Germany to-day are *white wines*, and most of the vineyards are given over to white wine production, though the amount of red wine made is more than is generally assumed. The two types of vine which are predominantly used for white wine production are the *Sylvaner* and the *Riesling*. There are many varieties and cross-breeds of these such as the *Müller-thurgau* and the *Scheu-rebe*. Nowadays practically all these vines are after careful selection grafted on American *Phylloxera-*immune stocks. Planting is done by propagation, as a rule from pre-selected shoots which have been allowed to develop roots over a period of two or three years, thereby giving quicker results. Experiments in crossings are constantly undertaken with the aim of achieving a frost-resistant vine which should at the same time produce wine of character and bouquet.

The Sylvaner succeeds in a moderately hot climate in heavy soil. It blossoms comparatively early, and the berries ripen earlier than those of the Riesling. The latter is a hardy plant; it can, in contrast with the Sylvaner, root well on rocky soil, which is important, as vines root deeply and can consequently put up with much less rain in summer than most other plants. As the Riesling grapes ripen late, warm and well-sited land, as described, is required. Riesling grapes are small, and hence the quantities harvested are less than those of the Sylvaner, but quality, bouquet and character make up for this deficiency. The Riesling, too, gives a wine that lasts better in bottle. In the Palatinate, the *Traminer* and *Gewürztraminer* can still be found, from which, in good vintages, mellow wines of a rare and highly pronounced bouquet are obtained.

Vineyards and Special Terms

A word now about the many varied names seen on German wine labels. In Bordeaux, to take an example, the entire crop from each vineyard is pressed and run off into large vats, and one single, homogeneous wine is made from it. A Château Talbot, for instance, is a wine of one vintage, of one estate, of one proprietor. German wines, however, with few exceptions, bear as principal description the name of the *parish*; each parish has many *vineyards*, each with its own name, and in most cases each vineyard is owned by *several proprietors*. About 75 per cent. of the vineyard territory is in the hands of small growers, but even in the rare case of a single monopoly, the following holds good.

The wines, though of the same *vineyard*, are frequently not equalised, or made homogeneous after the pressing, but are stored in different casks of about 130 gallons and upwards—on the Mosel in *Fuders* of about 215 gallons. Therefore not only the district and the vineyard must be considered when judging a wine, but also the parts of the vineyard, some of which may be more favourably situated as regards sunshine and soil, the age of the vines, etc.

Thus, one proprietor may gather, let us say, twelve casks of wine, each of a very different quality, yet launched upon the world bearing the same name. They will, however, fetch very different prices at the consequent auction sale, or from the shipper who acquired the crop. It would be wrong, therefore, to compare the price lists and conclude that a merchant is dearer because he quotes, say, a *Hattenheimer Nussbrunnen* at a higher price than another merchant, as this can only be decided upon quality.

Added to the geographical description on the label you may find also the name of the vine, for instance Riesling, and also words such as *Spätlese* and *Auslese*.

It is said that, in the seventeenth century, when the now "Schloss" Johannisberg was a Benedictine Monastery, its land-lord, the Bishop of Fulda, who lived a hundred miles away, had by some mismanagement overlooked ordering the start of the harvest. By the time permission arrived, the grapes had, due to the unusual autumn heat, shrunk into raisins. The poor monks in charge of the vineyard, used to gathering ripe grapes, were greatly disturbed and feared the worst. Much to the astonishment of all, however, it turned out to be an exceptionally grand wine, and thus began the custom of *Spätlese*—late-gathering.

Underlying this story is the fungus *Botrytis cinerea*, which can do harm as well as good. If the autumn is wet and the grapes unripe, it pierces the skins and causes grey rot—a grey powder on the skins which taints the wine. If dry weather and sunshine prevail, however, and the grapes are ripe, then it causes noble rot—*pourriture noble*—whereby the grape-juice evaporates and thus increases the grape-sugar content.

The word *Spätlese* is in itself, as the law stands, not a guarantee for quality; it merely indicates that the gathering of the grapes for that particular wine was postponed later than the general gathering. As such, it has been practised for a very long time. Homer alludes to it in his description of the garden of Alcinous. The Romans certainly knew the value of the various stages of gathering. And Goethe, after an excursion in the wine-lands in 1814, mentions the everlasting fight on the question which went on between poor and rich: "Those want the quantity, these the quality."

To show that his vineyard is planted with the famous Riesling, the grower frequently mentions this with the name of the wine; he may also add *Auslese* if the wine has been made from specially selected bunches of grapes. *Beeren-auslese* would imply that single berries have been selected and separated from the rest, probably for a small and very high-class cask of wine. *Trocken-beeren-auslese*, the culmination of the whole process, means that the wine has been made from a special selection of individually picked, over-matured, raisin-like berries. The original idea seems to have been the elimination of the pips from the berries, thereby making the wine sweeter, but this did not work well, as the pips give the wine its necessary tannin. Both *Beeren-Auslese* and *Trockenbeeren-Auslese* wines are genuinely called so if bouquet and taste show a raisin-like peculiarity different from other wines.

Labels, as we know them to-day, first appeared in the early nineteenth century, and then showed only such simple names as *Rheinwein*. These names were followed by that of the port of shipment. It was only much later that the minute descriptions mentioned were first used. Vineyard names, however, were used verbally long before they began to appear on labels. In a good many instances they point to some historical origin. On the Mosel, in particular, we find names which carry reminders of Roman times. They may indicate, as well, the name of a previous proprietor, of a landmark or some characteristic by which the vineyard could be recognised by the working people of the district.

The shape of the bottle used for German wines was, except in Franconia, first introduced in the early nineteenth century, but it was not till the last quarter of the century that the practice of maturing wines in bottle became frequent. Before that, wines had been matured for long periods in cask, and thereby acquired a dry taste of age in wood. The bottling of Rhine wines in *brown* and Mosel wines in *green* bottles became a habit at a somewhat later date.

There have always been, in Germany, many large and out-standing properties, but there are also, nowadays, many extensive and up-to-date factories and cellars owned by Vintagers' Associations or Co-operatives. Here the many small growers have cast in their lots together, though each continues to produce his own grapes. The grapes are delivered to the Co-operative, which pays by results, and undertakes both the manufacture and sale of the wine.

Though pests and leaf diseases are rarer these days than formerly, as means of destroying them have been developed, anti-disease precautions are specially necessary in a northern climate, and the expense of this proves considerable, with its effect on the final cost of the wine. For this reason, mass-produced wines have been eliminated in Germany, and the vineyard areas have been restricted to prevent vines being planted on soil unsuitable for high-class production. Quality cultivation is the only method by which German wines can justify the costs of production. This will be of even greater importance when the "European Market" starts and customs protection ceases.

The prices of German wines are influenced by considerations of bouquet, body and character—not by sweetness alone, without the other qualities. Bouquet and aroma, of course, cannot be expected in a relatively cheap wine, but from a certain stage onwards, given a natural inherent sweetness, the nose must also be given satisfaction. It can indeed be taken as a guide that, if a wine is not attractive in its bouquet it will not in the long run be satisfactory. Those led by sweetness alone will not obtain the best and soundest wines. It is not easy to give standard advice regarding the age at which these wines should be consumed. Technology and scientific knowledge of the nature of wine have within our time advanced to such a degree that, theoretically speaking, it is possible to have wines ready for consumption almost immediately after the gathering. This, however, does not allow the wine to acquire all desirable qualities; a wine, though technically bright, will grow in body and aroma and lose certain acids if granted gradual development. On the other hand, good wines—in particular white wines—can now successfully be obtained and consumed earlier than in the past. The lighter type, of ordinary and middle qualities, are often ready for consumption within a year or two after production; bigger wines will take longer and will, of course, keep longer too. But only the finest wines are worth keeping for a very long time.

The Palatinate

Let us begin our journey through the winelands right in the south, at the point where the Rheinpfalz—the Palatinate—starts, on the Alsatian frontier. While the wine made in this region is not remarkable, the scenery certainly is ! The view of the great woods, the Rhine valley and the backdrop of the Black Forest is enthralling.

Moving along the *Weinstrasse*—so-called because it leads through most of the Palatinate vineyards—we have, on the left, the forest of the Haardt mountains, which protects the plain from the east winds. From the name of the range the Palatinate wines are sometimes called Haardt wines. The *Weinstrasse* wanders through numerous little villages, with pretty, fan-worked houses decorated by climbing vines, and with vine-pergolas joining the houses. Sound wines, with both body and softness, can be found in the best places of the upper Haardt—places such as *Hambach*, near the chief Palatinate town of Neustadt, the latter with a considerable wine trade, and housing also the important Palatinate Viticultural Institute.

Climb the terraces close to the Haardt vineyards, and a vast panorama is revealed of almost all the middle Haardt. The abundance of chestnut-trees, almonds and figs prove its almost southern climate. Then the descent into the more gentle, plain-like country marks the entry into the richest part of the Palatinate. The impression of richness is strengthened by the state of the villages, by the many grand mansions, the number of cattle, and of course by the fertility of the vineyards themselves.

The Church has never had as strong an influence in the Palatinate as in other districts. The growers, therefore, became independent earlier than elsewhere, and this has had its influence on the character of the people, who show great individuality, a sound love of wine and a sense of humour. They do not mind their nickname, *Pälzer Krischer*—shriekers—and indeed justify it,

RHINE and MOSEL

TRIER

CONZ
OBEREMMEL
KANZEM
WILTINGEN
AYL
SERRIG

R. Saar

DETZEM
THORNICH

TRITTENHEIM
NEUMAGEN

PIESPORT
BRAUNEBERG

R. MOSEL

BERNCASTEL
GRAACH

COBLENZ

KREUZNACH

LANGENLONSHEIM

R. Nahe

R. RHINE

RHEINGAU

OCKENHEIM

BUDE HEIM
GEISENHEIM
WINKEL
ÖSTRICH

BINGEN

JOHANNISBERG
VOLLRADS
EBERBACH
KIEDRICH
RAUENTHAL

PALATINATE

HATTENHEIM

INGELHEIM

ERBACH

ELTVILLE

WIESBADEN

KALLSTADT
WACHENHEIM
RUPPERTSBERG
KONIGSBACH
GIMMELDINGEN

DURKHEIM
DEIDESHEIM
FORST
MUSSBACH
NEUSTADT
HAMBACH

BODENHEIM
NACKENHEIM
NIERSTEIN
OPPENHEIM
ALSHEIM
RECHTHEIM
WESTHOFEN
OSTHOFEN

MAINZ

R. RHINE

WORMS

MANNHEIM

FRANKFURT

N

as one of their parties in a *Weinstube* will prove! A Palatinate
poet put it quite well:

> We Palatinates are, I think,
> A strange race of curious humour;
> When we're merry—then we drink!
> When we're sad—then we drink more!

We pass Mussbach, Gimmeldingen and Königsbach, and, though
good wines are grown here, we are in a hurry to reach the paradise
of the Palatinate, which begins at Ruppertsberg. It would be un-
wise to try to classify all the places we pass by the quality of their
wines. Each of them has its own character, its own great wine, and
there are middling and ordinary wines produced as well. While
in the upper Haardt the predominant vine is the Sylvaner, we
now come to Riesling vineyards. In the heavy clay soil, and in the
full wealth of the southern sun, they produce wine of delicious
strong bouquet, coupled with a pronounced, though unobtrusive,
sweetness and body.

Ruppertsberg is a place of historic renown, a settlement of pre-
Christian origin, and later a Roman fort on an important junction.
The well-known *Hoheburg* vineyard takes its name from this
period. Other vineyards of renown are *Nussbien*, *Reiterpfad* and
Goldschmied. Only a short distance away is Deidesheim, a long,
stretched-out town, distinguished by names such as Buhl and
Bassermann-Jordan; the latter wrote the most important history
of German viticulture, while the Buhl family have been among the
best-known representatives of Palatinate viticulture for generations. Some of the most famous vineyards of Deidesheim are
Kieselberg, *Hofstück*, *Grain*, *Herrgottsacker*, *Mäushöhle* and *Leinhöhle*.

At Forst and nearby Wachenheim we find many famous properties, the most important vineyards of which are listed in full
in the appendix. They include the *Kirchenstück* and *Jesuitengarten*
at Forst, and the *Goldbächel* and *Gerümpel* at Wachenheim. When
we have considered these, we have mentioned the most outstanding growths of the Palatinate.

The climate of the Palatinate is the most favourable in Germany for the production of rich wines. Wines of outstanding years, such as 1934, '37, '45, '47, '49, '53, '59, '62, '64, '66, have a sweetness similar to Sauternes, though they are not so marked on the palate, as the fermentation is allowed to proceed further, and thereby they acquire more bouquet and fruit, while retaining a certain, though scarcely noticeable, acidity which combines elegance with sweetness.

The finest wines are made of Riesling grapes, though some rare casks of Traminer can also be obtained. These, however, are the exception, as the Riesling has the better chance on this schistous basalt soil. It need hardly be said that the best and richest wines are produced only in comparatively small quantities and fetch high prices. They can best be enjoyed with a suitable sweet or, better still, with fruit.

Though the Palatinate has been the scene of destruction in many wars, it has always recovered and rebuilt its towns. Thus many periods of architecture are represented, among them that little jewel of the late Renaissance—the town hall of Deidesheim.

One of the ravagers of the Palatinate was Napoleon's general, Mélac. He destroyed the castle of Heidelberg, where he set up his headquarters. A story goes that one day his soldiers captured a transport of wine in casks. The general tasted the wine and was so enraptured by its exceptional qualities that he did not rest until he had discovered its origin, which was Wachenheim. He engaged the head cellarman for himself and sent him to his Burgundy estates, to raise the wine production there to the same standard. When the good man's efforts failed, he was accused of sabotage, but pleaded that the sun and soil were the secret of the Palatinate's superiority. The victorious general then struck his colours, and became an admiring life-long customer of the wines of Wachenheim.

Now the area widens, while hills and forest recede into the vast vineyards of Dürkheim, the most extensive of the Palatinate.

Their *Michelsberg*, *Hochmess*, *Spielberg* and *Hoch-Benn* show a delightful lusciousness of body. The town is a spa, in fine surroundings, giving easy approach to all the Haardt forest. Nearby are
Ungstein and Kallstadt, which make big, powerful wines. Rather
lighter are those of Herxheim, at which place we reach the end
of the middle Haardt. Passing onwards through many vineyards
in the low valley, where both red and white wines are made, we
reach Worms.

Rhenish Hessia

Worms, a city of ancient date and fame, became an episcopal
diocese at the beginning of the eleventh century, and embraced
within its walls numerous monasteries and widespread ecclesias-
tical properties. The bishopric reached well into the Palatinate
and Rhenish Hessia.

On the northern outskirts of the town once stood a chapel
which was later replaced by the Gothic *Liebfrauenkirche*—the
Church of the Madonna. Vineyards were planted here which,
for centuries before the secularisation in the Napoleonic age,
belonged in part to the monasteries. They were in part ecclesias-
tical grants—*Stiftungen*. From these vineyards comes the name of
Liebfraumilch or *Liebfrauenmilch*, probably the most famous of
German wines. Its name can be traced back several hundred years,
to a time when vineyard names were still not in existence and the
wine trade was in the hands of the Church. Though the name
undoubtedly owes its origin to these vineyards, it appears that at
an early date it was applied to wine from the wider area of Worms,
outside the small extent of the *Liebfrauenstift*, in the same way as
river ports gave their name to wines shipped from them, irres-
pective of origin. The Liebfrauenstift itself gives its name to the
actual growth of its own vineyards (*Liebfrauenstiftswein*), and may
not be used for any other wines. The Liebfrauenstift has a pre-
dominance of Rieslings—old, ungrafted Rieslings at that—for it
is one of the few areas so far unaffected by *Phylloxera*. Well-

known parts of Liebfrauenstift are *Klostergarten* and *Kirchenstück*.

In the fertile surroundings of Worms, where the soil is heavy and loamy, we find a number of important wine-places, such as Westhofen, Osthofen, Bechtheim, Mettenheim, Alsheim. Passing along the route from Worms to Mainz, through Dienheim and Guntersblum, we reach the beautifully situated town of Oppenheim. From its height we gain a wide view of a realm of vineyards, of whole hill-slopes washed by an unbroken flow of vines, and of the distant Rhine valley. The town of Oppenheim is crowned with a delightful monument of Gothic art—the Katharinen Kirche.

The following are the most outstanding vineyards of Oppenheim: *Herrenberg, Sackträger, Goldberg, Krötenbrunnen, Reisekahr.* The wines of these domains are full-bodied and well-ripened.

On the short trip from Oppenheim to Nierstein, we notice the change of colour of the soil—a red loam gives a distinctive appearance to the Nierstein and Nackenheim vineyards. Many of the vineyards hereabouts were, in the Middle Ages, Crown properties which later passed to the Church, and some vineyard names remind us of these times. The *Hintersaal* at Nierstein, for instance, refers to a Carolingian hall that once stood there. Other outstanding growths include *Auflangen, Rehbach, Hipping, Orbel, Brudersberg, Glöck* and *Pettental*. While ordinary table wines are produced at Nierstein, there is no place to equal its finest wines, which can develop a delightfully smooth and even sweet, nutty taste which makes them ideal as great dessert wines.

Add to the above the names of Nackenheim, with its *Fenchelberg* and *Roterberg*, and Bodenheim with the *Westrum* and *Leistenberg*, and we have then named all the outstanding wine-places of this part of Rheinhessen.

There is, however, in another corner of this district, a wine city of great distinction—Bingen. The town is situated on the Rhine where it bends to the north, and where the Nahe joins the great river. Its *Rochusberg, Eisel* and *Schwätzerchen* are full-bodied wines of character, while the *Scharlachberg* of Büdesheim, a town incorporated with Bingen, is equally great.

The Nahe

The charming valley of the Nahe produces two different types of wine; a heavy, full-bodied wine like some of the Rhenish Hessians, which are produced from soft vines from the loamy soil of the lower river valley, and a wine much like a Mosel, produced from Rieslings grown on the gravel and slate soil as at Kreuznach.

The first type of wine is made at Langenlonsheim, Odernheim and Ockenheim. The second comes from Kreuznach—with its famed *Kauzenberg*—Norheim, Niederhausen, Waldböckelheim and Schloss Böckelheim. These Mosel-type wines need very careful treatment, and can, by *Auslese*, attain outstanding quality. In

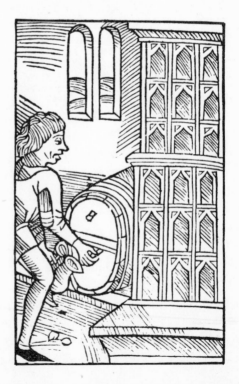

Kreuznach, a fine health resort with an important shipping trade, the many restaurants offer a wonderful range of these wines, and offer maps of the area.

Returning via Ingelheim, the best red wine centre of Rhein-hesse, to Mainz, we reach a centre of the Rhenish Hessian trade. Even-in early times there was an archbishop resident at Mainz who, in his rôle of Prince Elector, exerted a great influence on viticulture, both in Rheinhessen and in the Rheingau. His cathedral chapter at one time possessed an excellent part of the nearby Hochheim vineyards, from which date comes the vine-yard name of *Dom Dechaney* (Cathedral Deanery).

Hochheim, though on the Main, is, by nature of its wines, rightly ranged with the Rheingau. Whether its name has been the source of the word *Hock* is not definitely established, but it is probable, since Hochheim, as the shipping centre for the important trade of Frankfurt, may have given its name to wines not grown on the spot, before designations of origin came into general use.

The Rheingau

The Rheingau extends from Nieder-Walluf (Schierstein), near Wiesbaden, to Lorch. Riesling vines predominate, and they succeed particularly well in the slate and silica soil, which turns in places to gravel. The climate helps them too, for in spite of the northerly situation it is mild, and the beautiful Taunus mountains shelter the region from the winds. Wine, indeed, is made and enjoyed in ideal surroundings, on historic ground stamped with relics of a long tradition of civilisation.

From the twelfth century onwards the Church expanded its control over the Rheingau, and right up to the Renaissance exercised a wealth of power, magnificent evidence of which still remains. One of the greatest religious figures, a Schönbrun, Archbishop of Mainz, is still represented by descendants who own vineyards all over the Rheingau. Historic places abound. Eltville, once capital of the Gau, is rich in such buildings; even to-day many distinguished wine producers have their residences and estates in the nearby district.

Some distance up the slopes of the hills lies Rauenthal, whose *Siebenmorgen*, *Rothenberg* and *Pfaffenpfad* vineyards produce full-bodied wines of pronounced flavour. On the next chain of hills is Kiedrich, with its famous and beautiful St. Michael's Chapel, a late Gothic fifteenth-century building. An Englishman, Sir John Sutton, restored it at his own expense, as also the church, which houses the oldest organ in Germany. Sir John, who died in 1873, is well remembered for these generous deeds. Kiedrich has very delicate, elegant wines of great distinction, from such renowned vineyards as *Gräfenberg*, *Langenberg*, *Sandgrube* and *Wasserrose*.

At Erbach, in the valley, one of the most famous of German wines is made. This is the *Markobrunn*, so called from the little well that marked the border-line of the commune. Equally good wines are produced in Erbach's *Brühl*, *Honigberg* and *Rheinhell* vineyards. The nearby town of Hattenheim is proud also of its fine wines, which come from the vineyards of *Nussbrunnen*, *Wissel-brunn* and *Engelsmannberg*. These wines are firmer than those of Erbach.

From Hattenheim, by a steady rise through the vineyards, we arrive at Kloster Eberbach, which lies hidden by hills till one is almost at its gates. It is in every way the most impressive and important monument of olden times in the Rheingau. Founded as a Cistercian Monastery by Bernard of Clairvaux in the early twelfth century, it remained such until its secularisation by Napoleon. Most of the extensive buildings are still in existence and, with the many fine sculptures which they contain, form a great historical document of Gothic and Renaissance times. A rare collection of old wine-presses, dating back to the sixteenth century, can now be seen in the so-called Black Cellar.

From the twelfth century onwards lay brethren planted vines on the *Steinberg*, the wines of which gained a great reputation even in medieval times. These Steinberg wines have unique characteristics, especially a lightness and a bouquet of lilac. Their *Cabinet wines*, and in particular their *Beerenauslese*, reach a very high quality. The word *Cabinet* originally referred to wines from the estate kept in the private cellars of certain potentates, and is now given to estate-bottled wines which attain a certain minimum price at the auction sales.

Cabinet wines are also produced at *Schloss Johannisberg*, a compact estate situated high above the Rhine valley. A Benedictine Monastery from the middle of the twelfth century, it was presented, shortly after secularisation, by Napóleon to General Kellermann, the victor of Valmy. In 1815, at the Congress of Vienna, it was given by the Austrian monarch to Metternich, on condition of a tithe to the Austrian Crown.

The Schloss vineyards were severely damaged by *Phylloxera*, but have been successfully replanted so that the best wines still show great bouquet and firmness. Wines almost as good are made in the adjoining estates of *Hölle* and *Kerzenstück*, but the *Dorf Johannisberg* wines, which come from vines grown on the lower slopes do not, on the average, attain these standards.

Descending from Dorf Johannisberg, we reach Winkel, a favourite wine-place of Goethe's, with its *Honigberg*, *Oberberg* and *Dachsberg* vineyards. The route then goes through Mittelheim, Oestrich, with its luscious wines from the *Lenchen*, *Doosberg* and *Kellerberg* estates, to Hallgarten, with the famous wines of *Händelberg*, *Schönhell* and *Deitelsberg*.

Just before Winkel a road branches off and rises to an even more famous wine-place, *Schloss Vollrads*. This moated castle has been in the hands of the Matuschka family for over six centuries, and the tradition of great wine-making is carried on by the present Count, a prominent figure in viticultural circles.

The next place on the Rhine road is Geisenheim, with its well-known *Rothenberg*, *Decker* and *Kosackenberg* estates. There is also a well-known Viticultural College and Research Institute here. Passing through the town, we come to the imposing "Berg" of

Rüdesheim. The great wines of this place are grown on rocky terraces above the river. The vineyards here bore the brunt of the attack in the last war, and suffered badly from bombing. The costly and difficult work of restoring has, however, obliterated all traces of the damage.

And so we come to the end of the fine white wine area of the Rheingau. Some of the finest white wines in the world have been mentioned in the last page or two, and it would be unfair to single out any for special mention. The Auslese and Beerenauslese, of course, are finer than the ordinary quality wines, and command the respect of all wine-lovers.

The Mosel

The Mosel, with its two important tributaries, the Saar and the Ruwer, falls into three distinct areas: the Upper Mosel, which produces small wines; the Middle Mosel, from Trier to Enkirch, which with the Saar and Ruwer produces half of all the Mosel wines and its best; and the Lower Mosel, from north-east of Enkirch to Coblenz.

Trier was the gateway city through which the Romans entered Germany. Later it was the centre from which the Church extended its influence. As both the Romans and the Church were interested in viticulture, the city has been associated with wine-making for a very long time indeed, and is steeped in tradition.

As the Saar and the Ruwer join the Mosel near Trier, we shall take them first, following the courses of the rivers and mentioning the important wines as we reach their vineyards.

The idyllic Saar valley is entirely in German territory. Beginning at Serrig, which has important State vineyards, we must mention Ayl with its outstanding *Herrenberg*, Ockfen with its *Bockstein* and *Geisberg*, Wiltingen with *Kupp*, *Schlangengraben* and even more famous *Scharzhofberg*, Oberemmel with the *Rosenberg*, *Agritiusberg* and *Scharzberg*, Kanzem with the *Kelterberg*, Krettnach

A Rhenish glass of the 16th century

The pleasures of wine

Colour

The pleasures of wine

Bouquet

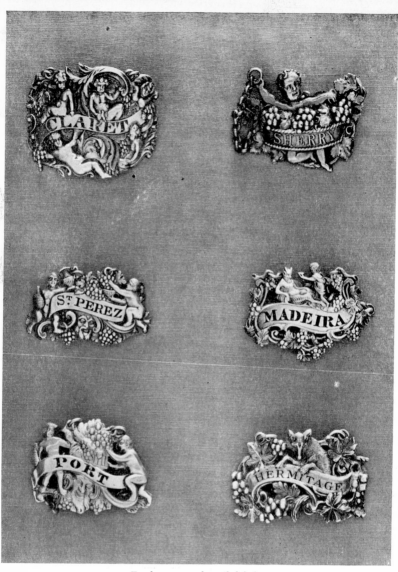

Further examples of labels

with *Euchariusberg*, Wawern with its *Herrenberg*, and finally, with Conz, the *Falkenstein*.

On the Ruwer let us mention Avelsbach, Casel, Waldrach, Grünhaus and, last but not least, Eitelsbach with the *Karthäuser-Hofberg*, which owes its name to the fact that for five centuries it was owned by the Carthusians. All these Saar and Ruwer wines are very delicate, with a highly pronounced, delightful bouquet.

The wines of the Middle Mosel are bigger, and have a different, crisp aroma. They can all, however, attain a great mellowness and rich, velvet taste, and owe their flavour to exclusive Riesling cultivation on an air-slaked slate soil of great variety.

The hills banking the Mosel are steep, often too steep for either animals or machines to be used in cultivation. The vineyards change from side to side of the river, as it twists tortuously through the mountainous landscape, in order to obtain the best of the sun. Famous places on this part of the Mosel are Detzem and Thörnich, Trittenheim with its *Falkenberg* and *Laurentiusberg*, Neumagen with its *Rosengärtchen*, Dhron, Piesport—with the outstanding *Goldtröpfchen*—Wintrich, Brauneberg with the *Hasen-läufer*, *Bürgerslay* and *Juffer*, Lieser with its often excellent *Nieder-berg*, and, finally, the provincial town of Bernkastel.

Bernkastel is an attractive town, but its fame lies in its wines— the *Schlossberg*, the *Badstube* and the famous *Doktor*. The story goes that a Trier Prince Elector fell ill when living at the castle, and, medical help having failed, was cured when he drank this par-ticular wine. From that time onward it was considered the best "doctor."

Close to Bernkastel is Graach, with its supreme *Himmelreich*, Zeltingen, far too little known for its great products from the *Schlossberg* and other fine vineyards, Uerzig, which makes even more luscious wines in great years from its *Würzgarten*, Wehlen with its *Sonnenuhr*, and Erden with its *Busslei*, *Treppchen* and *Herrenberg*. We have now mentioned the Great Lords of the Mosel.

Good also are the wines from the town of Traben-Trarbach, which is situated on both sides of the river, from Enkirch, with its *Steffensberg*, and finally from Reil. And there we will leave the Mosel, though the *Krampen* wines—so-called from the "cramp iron" bend of the river—are light, soft and attractive, and the wines of the Untermosel are pleasant without distinction.

Franconia

On the River Main, quite apart from the districts so far mentioned, the wines of Franconia are produced. The production of wines in this region was started by the Carolingians about the end of the eighth century, and now flourishes on the winding banks of the river and its small tributaries. A soil of shell and lime, with red chalk to the west, is good ground for the Rieslings and Traminer vines, though the Sylvaner is also grown.

The main wine-places are Dettelsbach, Kitzingen, Rödelsee, Escherndorf, Sommerach, Randersacker, and the district around Würzburg. At this last, on the Steinberg, the finely sited hill facing the town, is made the *Steinwein*, which is rivalled only by the *Leisten* and *Schalksberg*, grown and produced on nearby slopes. The *Schlossberg* is a wine of slightly poorer quality.

These wines are big, with body and character. The Stein, according to a poem, "warms, makes cheerful, nourishes and heals"! In Germany Franconian wines have the sole privilege of being bottled in *Bocksbeutels*—flagon-shaped bottles of attractive appearance.

On Drinking Wines

German white wines should be drunk cool—cooler in summer than winter. In general, the sweeter the wine the cooler it should be drunk. The cork should be drawn a short time before the meal. In Germany, lighter wines are drunk as apéritifs, and in the evening after dinner.

Any Mosel or Rhine wine can be drunk throughout a meal; if, however, one wine only is served, it seems better to have one that is not too luscious, as it might get tiring. A luscious, or moderately luscious, wine appeals better to the palate if it is preceded by a light, dry wine, and is then brought on with the roast, poultry or game—or even fruit. Wines are always best served in order from the poorest to the greatest, so that each one exposes the qualities of its successor. A dinner on a big scale, consequently, might start with a light Mosel or dry Rheingau with the hors-d'œuvres, be followed by a moderately rich wine, a good, but not too good, not too sweet Liebfraumilch or similar Rhine wine for example, and then be brought to a close with the main dish and a luscious and full-flavoured Rhine wine from any district.

Mosel wines, of course, can be found big enough so that an entire meal can be taken up with them, always serving the lighter wine before the bigger one. German wines, too, can be interchanged with French. A meal could start with a light dry Mosel, change to a claret or red burgundy with the meat or poultry, and end with a fine Spätlese or Auslese from the Gau or Palatinate.

These are merely suggestions, for no hard-and-fast rule should hamper one's own imagination. Smell and sip your wines with careful attention, and this will help you to remember them, and then to work out a sequence for them at a meal. This is the sort of knowledge with which one can afford to break "rules," and thereby give and receive a great deal of pleasure.

Bibe multis annis are the words inscribed on a fourth-century Cologne goblet—"Drink for many years." This implies drinking with wisdom, in moderation, as a contribution to health and spirit, as a permanent habit—a habit acquired by enjoying what we drink. This book has attempted to help you on your way to that full enjoyment.

HOCK

HOCK AND MOSEL

Key to the wine areas: P=Palatinate; H=Rhenish Hessia; G=Rheingau; N=Nahe; M=Mosel; S=Saar; R=Ruwer; F=Franconia; B=Baden.

Area	Name	Outstanding Vineyard
B	Affenthal (red wine)	
	Ahr (red wine)	
M	Aldegund	
H	Alsheim	Friedrichsberg; Goldberg; Hahl; Sonnenberg
P	Alsterweiler	
G	Assmannshausen (red wine)	
R	Avelsbach	Domavelsbach; Hammerstein
S	Ayl	Herrenberg; Kupp
H	Bechtheim	Geiersberg
M	Beilstein	
M	Bernkastel	Doktor; Amorpfad; Kirchengrube; Rosenberg; Schlossberg
H	Bingen	Eisel; Rochusberg
H	Bingen-Büdesheim	Scharlachberg
N	Böckelheim	
H	Bodenheim	Kahlenberg; Leimen
M	Brauneberg	Falkenberg; Hasenläufer; Juffer
N	Bretzenheim	
M	Briedel	
M	Bruttig	
S	Canzem	Altenberg; Kelterberg
R	Casel	Niessgen
M	Cochem	
S	Conz	Falkenstein
S	Crettnach	Euchariusberg
M	Cues	Weissenstein
P	Deidesheim	Grain; Hohenmorgen; Hofstück; Herrgottsacker; Kranzler; Kieselberg; Vogelsang
F	Dettelbach	
M	Detzem	
M	Dhron	Hengelsberg; Hofberg; Sängerei
H	Dienheim	Guldenmorgen

Area	Name	Outstanding Vineyard
P	Dürkheim	Feuerberg; Michelsberg; Spiegelberg
P	Edenkoben	
R	Eitelsbach	Karthäuser-Hofberg
G	Eltville	Grimmen; Langenstuck
M	Enkirch	Steffensberg
G	Erbach	Brühl; Honigberg; Markobrunn
M	Erden	Busslei; Treppchen
F	Escherndorf	
S	Filzen	
P	Forst	Fleckinger; Freundstück; Jesuitengarten; Kirchenstück; Ungeheuer; Musenhang; Pechstein
H	Gaubickelheim	
G	Geisenheim	Decker; Kosackenberg; Rothenberg
P	Gimmeldingen	Meerspinne
M	Graach	Dompropst; Himmelreich; Josephshof
R	Grünhaus	Maximin Grünhaus
H	Guntersblum	Himmelthal; Steig
P	Haardt	
G	Hallgarten	Deitelsberg; Hendelberg; Schönhell
P	Hambach	
G	Hattenheim	Engelmannsberg; Nussbrunnen; Wisselbrunnen
P	Herxheim	
G	Hochheim	Bettelmann; Daubhaus; Dom Dechaney; Kirchenstück
G	Johannisberg	Erntebringer; Hölle; Klaus; Schlossberg
M	Josephshof (see Graach)	
P	Kallstadt	Horn; Nill; Saumagen
H	Kempten	
M	Kesten	
G	Kiedrich	Gräfenberg; Sandgrube; Wasserrose
M	Kinheim	
F	Kitzingen	
P	Königsbach	Idig; Bender; Rolandsberg
N	Kreuznach	Mönchberg; Schloss Kauzenberg; Narrenkappe
M	Kröv	

Area	Name	Outstanding Vineyard
N	Langenlonsheim	
H	Laubenheim	
H	Liebfrauenstift (*see* Worms)	
M	Lieser	Kirchberg; Niederberg; Paulsberg
G	Lorch	Honigberg
H	Ludwigshöhe	
P	Maikammer	
M	Maring	
B	Markgräfler	
G	Markobrunner (*see* Erbach)	
H	Mettenheim	Michelsberg; Hellborn
M	Minheim	
G	Mittelheim	Edelmann; Oberberg
M	Mühlheim	
N	Münster am Stein	
P	Mussbach	
H	Nackenheim	Fenchelberg; Rothenberg; Kirchberg
M	Neumagen	Engelgrube; Rosengärtchen
P	Neustadt	Grain; Vogelsang
M	Niederemmel	
N	Niederhausen	
H	Nierstein	Auflangen; Brudersberg; Hipping; Glöck; Kranzberg; Pettental; Rehbach; Spiegelberg
N	Norheim	
S	Oberemmel	Agritiusberg; Scharzberg; Rosenberg
H	Oberingelheim (red wine)	
H	Ockenheim	
S	Ockfen	Bockstein; Geisberg
G	Oestrich	Doosberg; Eiserberg; Eiserweg; Kellerberg; Lenchen; Pflänzer
M	Ohligsberg (*see* Wintrich)	
H	Oppenheim	Goldberg; Krötenbrunnen; Reisekahr; Sackträger
M	Piesport	Falkenberg; Goldtröpfchen; Michelsberg
F	Randersacker	
G	Rauenthal	Langenstück; Pfaffenberg; Siebenmorgen; Wagenkehr

Area	Name	Outstanding Vineyard
M	Reil	Goldlay; Mulay
N	Rüdesheim	
G	Rüdesheim	Bischofsberg; Bronnen; Rottland; Schlossberg
P	Ruppertsberg	Goldschmied; Hoheburg; Nussbien; Reiterpfad
P	St. Martin	
H	Scharlachberger (*see* Bingen)	
S	Scharzberg (*see* Oberemmel)	
S	Scharzhofberg (*see* Wiltingen)	
N	Schloss Böckelheim	Kupfergrube; Muhlberg
G	Schloss Vollrads	
S	Serrig	Hindenburglei; Kupp; Vogelsang; Würtzberger
G	Steinberg	
F	Steinwein (*see* Würzburg)	
M	Thörnich	
M	Traben	Königsberg; Würzgarten
M	Trarbach	Schlossberg
M	Trier	Augenscheiner; Tiergärtner
M	Trittenheim	Altärchen; Laurentiusberg; Sonnteil
M	Uerzig	Würzgarten
P	Ungstein	Herrenberg; Spielberg
M	Valwig	
P	Wachenheim	Böhlig; Goldbächel; Luginsland; Gerümpel
N	Waldböckelheim	
R	Waldrach	Kronlay; Mariaberg; Hubertusberg
S	Wawern	Herrenberg
M	Wehlen	Klosterlay; Münzlay; Sonnenuhr
H	Westhofen	
S	Wiltingen	Kupp; Scharzhofberg; Schlangengraben; Rosenberg
N	Windesheim	
G	Winkel	Dachsberg; Honigberg; Oberberg
M	Winningen	
M	Wintrich	Geierslay; Ohligsberg
N	Winzenheim	

Area	Name	Outstanding Vineyard
H	Worms	Liebfrauenstift
F	Würzburg	Leisten; Steinwein
M	Zell	Schwarze Katz
M	Zeltingen	Himmelreich; Rotlay; Schlossberg

Chapter Eleven

The Wines of Italy

ITALY produces more wine than any other country in Europe except France. Probably, too, the country not only makes more wine, but more wines as well, because their number and variety are almost endless. Most of them are pleasant, and many of them are good. But no sustained attempt has ever been made to raise the quality of Italian wines to a par with the Classed Growths of France or the great wines of Germany. This is a pity, for at least two reasons: one, because with proper care and treatment, many Italian wines could rival claret and Barsac; two, because without such care, nearly all Italian wines lack the breed and stamina to withstand the strains of travel and the cold of Britain. At present, only a few Italian wines can travel, and these are not always the best. Even these few, alas, have an unhappy habit of acquiring a nasty taste after a short time in an English cellar.

The vineyards of Italy extend from the Swiss frontier to the shores of Sicily. White wines are made everywhere, but, in general, no good red wines are made to the south of Tuscany. Indeed, it is fairly safe to say that the best wines come from the northern provinces. Whether this is due to climatic and soil conditions, or to the fact that the north is more advanced than the south, it would be hard to say.

Nearly all the wines of Italy are beverage wines, table wines. At the present stage of their development they do not mature appreciably in bottle and have not a long life. The more ordinary wines are well worth drinking before they reach three years old, and even the better grades are at their best at about five years.

Wine should be judged by its bouquet, its colour and its taste, not by the attractiveness of its bottle. A plain wine bottle is less attractive than a Chianti flask, but this does not make Chianti a better wine than, say, Barolo. It is important to mention this, because, due to its flask, Chianti is about the only Italian wine known in England, other than Frascati.

If the Italian wines that are shipped abroad are rarely great wines, this does not mean that really fine wine is not made in Italy. The writer can give assurance that it is, but, unfortunately, only in small quantities usually reserved for the owner of the estate. A *Vinsanto*, from a private estate in Tuscany, demands comparison with really good *Fino* sherry, and a really good Chianti, drunk in Italy, can hold its own with most red wines.

Italian wines once had greater popularity in Britain than they have to-day. Trade relations between England and Tuscany encouraged the import of Italian wines, and the *Vernaccia* wines of Florence were very popular in England from Chaucer's day right down to the end of the eighteenth century, and *Florence*, *Montecatini*, and *Est Est Est* are fairly common on English wine labels.

The most famous red wine of Italy is *Chianti*. It comes from Tuscany, from a defined region near Siena. There is no specially prescribed vine from which the wine is made, and, indeed, many different varieties are used. This means that no two Chiantis are alike, and that the wine varies greatly in quality. It is refreshing and pleasant in the hot Tuscan summer, but the Chianti imported to Britain is nothing spectacular. It is often rather harsh, crude and without subtlety. *Brolio Chianti* is considered the best. *Chianti Ruffino*, a mass-produced wine from Pontassieve, is also commonly found.

From Tuscany also comes *Montepulciano*, a red wine which can be quite good, and has a famous reputation to maintain.

The northern provinces of Lombardy, Piedmont and Veneto make the finest red wines of Italy. From Veneto, from vineyards around Lake Garda, comes a good dry wine. Its finest name is

Valpolicella, probably the nearest thing in Italy to a vintage claret. *Bardolino*, from the same region, is also good.

Farther north, in Sondrio, the wines of the *Valtellina* are very pleasant. The best-known, *Sassella*, has more bouquet than most Italian wine, and has, as well, a beautiful colour.

From a limited area in Piedmont, called Le Langhe, comes *Barolo*, held by many to be the best red wine of Italy. It is certainly better than most Chianti.

A great deal of red wine from the northern provinces is made and sold under the names of the vine from which it comes. The two best-known examples are *Nebbiolo* and *Barbera*. If the relation between them is not quite that of Pinot to Gamay, it is certain that, while the Nebbiolo can produce a fine red wine, the Barbera rarely rises above an *ordinaire*. Neither of these vine names should be taken as being an indication of quality, as, say, an Alsace *Riesling*. Where a good wine is made from these vines, it will bear the vineyard name, after the name of the vine.

Good white wines are made all over Italy. From Veneto comes *Soave*, a pleasant, dry wine. The Piedmontese *Caluso,* on the other hand, is sweet and luscious, and is made from over-ripened grapes, sun-dried on straw. From Central Italy comes *Orvieto*, a wine with great possibilities, given careful treatment. The sweet Orvieto, called *abboccato*, is preferable to the dry version. Orvieto is bottled in flasks, like Chianti.

From the Montefiascone region of Latium comes the famed *Est Est Est*, a golden Moscatello wine of distinction. The story behind its name is well known. A church dignitary, journeying through Italy, was possessed of an appreciative palate. To save time, he sent his servant into the villages ahead of him, with orders to sample the local wine and to write his opinion, in Latin, on the tavern door. If it was good, he wrote "Est" (it is); if bad, "Non Est" (it is not). When the bishop came to Montefiascone, he found written "Est Est Est"!

From the vineyards around Foggia—much devastated during

the war—come two good white wines, both dry, called *San Severo* and *Torre Giulia*. Rather less good are the well-known wines of Campania, *Capri*, a sweetish wine made mainly on the island of Ischia, and *Lacrima Cristi*, from the lower slopes of Vesuvius.

Asti Spumante is the Italian champagne. It is a sweet, sparkling wine made from Moscato grapes. It was formerly made from Nebbiolo, at least according to Stendhal, who praises it in the *Charterhouse of Parma*.

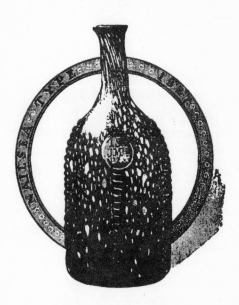

Index

abboccato, 195
Affenthal, 188
Agritiusberg, 184, 190
Ahr, 188
Aigrots, Les, 90
Albariza, (soil) 151, (vineyards) 153
Albert Grivaux, 101
Albillo (vine), 152
Aldegund, 188
Aligoté, 83
Aloxe-Corton, 85, 90–1, 98, 100
Alsace, 22, 115, 121, (map) 123
Alsheim, 179, 188
Alsterweiler, 188
Altärchen, 191
Altenberg, 188
Ambarès, 69
Ambes, 69
American (vine) 132–3, 152
Amontillado, 151, 158–9, 164
Amoroso, 164
Amorpfad, 188
Amoureuses, Les, 88, 97
Angelus, Ch. L', 72
Anjou, 22, 119
apéritifs, 186
Appellation d'Origine Contrôlée, 47, 52–3, 62
Arbois, 121
Arenas, (soil) 151
Armagnae, 122, 124; Bas-, Fin-, Grand-, Haut-, Petit, 124
Arsac, 58, 68, 71
Artisan growths, 50
Assmannshausen, 188
Asti Spumante, 196
Auflangen, 179, 190
Augenscheiner, 191
Auslese, 171, 184
Ausone, Ch., 60, 69, 72
'Australian Port', 128
Auxey-Duresses, 100, 101
Aux Savennières, 120
Aux Vergelesses, 98
Avaux, Les, 90
Avelsbach, 185, 188
Avignon, 116
Ayala, 112
Ayguemorte, 76
Ayl, 184, 188

Baden, 188, 190
Badstube, 185
Balestard la Tonnelle, Ch., 72
Barbera, 195
Bardolino, 195
Baret, Ch., 76
Barolo, 194
Barros (soil), 151
Barsac, 64, 69, 74, 75; First, Second, Growths, 75; official classification, 75
Bas-Armagnac, 124
Bas-Médoc, 58
Bastardo, 125
Batailley, Ch., 69, 71
Bâtard-Montrachet, 92, 100
Baudot, 101
Bayle (Guiraud), Ch., 74
Bay Peste, du, 101
Beaujeu, 95
Beaujolais, 22, 80, 93–5, 99; name, 95
Beaulieu, 120
Beaune, 90–101; Chorey les-, 98; Côte de, 8, (map) 89, 90, 98–9, 100; Hospices de, 90, 98; Savigny-les-, 98, 101
Beauregard, Ch., 73
Beauroy, 99
Beauséjour (Dufau), Beauséjour (Fagouet), Ch., 72
Beautiran, 76
Bechtheim, 177, 188
Beeren-auslese, 171–2, 183–4
Beilstein, 188
Belair, Ch., 72
Belgrave, Ch., 69, 71
Bellevue, Ch., 72
Bender, 189
Bernkastel, 185, 188
Bertolo, S.A., 165
Bessards, Les, 118
Bettelmann, 189
Beugnon, 99
Beychevelle, Ch., 69, 71
Bienvenue-Bâtard-Montrachet, 100
Bingen, 179, 188
Bingen-Büdesheim, 188
Bischofsberg, 191
blanc-fumé, 120
Blanchots, 93, 99
Blayais, 62